The Best of
House Doctor

First impression as a paperback published in Great Britain in 2004 by
Collins, an imprint of
HarperCollins*Publishers*
77–85 Fulham Palace Road
London W6 8JB

The Collins website address is www.collins.co.uk

Collins is a registered trademark of HarperCollins*Publishers* Ltd.

This material originally appeared in the House Doctor books by Ann Maurice with Fanny Blake.
This volume compiled and edited by Barbara Dixon for Essential Works.
Designed by Barbara Saulini and Paul Collins for Essential Works.

www.housedoctor.co.uk

09 08 07 06 05 04 03
7   6   5   4   3   2   1

A catalogue record for this book is available from the British Library.

ISBN: 0 00 717560 4

Printed and bound in Italy.

The Best of
House
Doctor

Ann Maurice

CONTENTS

INTRODUCTION

It's nearly impossible to believe that eight years have gone by since I first introduced the concept of 'home staging' to the British audience on national television. And while writing this introduction, I am also in the middle of filming the sixth series of the House Doctor programme for Channel 5. This new series brings the total number of programmes to seventy-two and, amazingly, the viewing audience continues to grow larger each year.

What is the secret of the 'House Doctor's' success? I think it is down to several things: For one thing, people in Britain love to snoop. Just take a look at the tabloids – they are filled with the inside 'scoop' on people's private lives. Viewers love being able to peer behind closed doors into other people's houses, something they rarely get a chance to do in real life. Also, the viewing audience loves watching the homeowners being judged by a jury of their 'peers'. There is a certain amount of Schadenfreude involved here. It makes them somehow feel better about themselves to see the contributors squirm and flinch at the viewers' comments. Thirdly, they all seem to appreciate my 'straight-talking, tell it like it is' manner. I guess being American, what I consider to be a normal way of dealing with people and situations seems to be rather extreme in comparison to British reserve.

In reality, I am the one who is saying exactly what the viewing audience is thinking. And finally, people are now more than ever interested in their homes, not only as a place to live, but as an investment as well.

When I first introduced the concept of 'home staging' here, I met with a lot of resistance. People did not understand the rationale behind the idea of spending money on one's home before selling. It seemed to make no sense at all. However, now, due to the many property programmes on television, articles in magazines and newspapers, and the accessibility of information on the Internet, the general public has become much more aware of the advantages of a properly presented home. It has become general practice among many sellers throughout Britain to follow my lead when selling their homes.

In the past six years, property values in Britain have soared, doubling and even trebling in certain areas. It is no wonder that the public has sat up and taken notice, paying close attention to every nuance of information regarding their most important lifetime investment. This also explains why the concept of 'home staging' has become so popular. So popular, in fact, that due to popular demand, I have begun to teach courses in the 'how to's' of home staging. People from all over Britain have attended my course, as well as from the Continent, the USA and Canada – all eager to learn my successful technique. The participants have been a real mix of people… interior designers and estate agents who are interested in adding this skill to their repertoire, those who are thinking of selling their own homes, and those who are simply curious about the process. There is a group of those delegates who are serious about making a career out of home staging and my plan for the future is to train a core group of serious and capable students to a higher level and create an 'Ann Maurice' network of competent home stagers throughout Britain.

My first three books House Doctor, House Doctor Quick Fixes and Instant Makeovers have sold like hotcakes. I am thrilled about this, not merely because of the obvious, but also because I feel as though I have been able to help numerous people survive one of the most difficult and stressful events of a lifetime – moving house. This gives me much personal satisfaction. By following my simple instructions, people have been able to add value to their homes (whether selling or not) and experience a 'smooth move'.

This latest book is a compilation of what I consider to be the 'best of House Doctor'. It takes the reader on a journey through the home, room by room, much the way that a prospective buyer would walk through to view it. It also includes step-by-step projects, advice on how to make the most of a home's existing features, and solutions for those nagging problem areas with which we are all too familiar. The contents of this book make it easy to 'cut to the quick' and rapidly discover what it takes to present your home in true 'Ann Maurice' style to get that quick sale, or simply to make it more comfortable and liveable. It could easily be called the 'Ann Maurice House Doctor Bible' and deserves a space on the shelf of every homeowner in Britain.

Happy reading!

Ann Maurice
www.housedoctor.co.uk

Whether you are just about to phone your estate agent to begin the process of selling your home or have been trying for some time unsuccessfully to get that sale, I encourage you to read this book. By following my simple, commonsense tips you will be able to get the highest and best price for your home and get it fast.

What is this mysterious secret that I bring with me from across the Pond? It is called 'home staging', and has become hugely successful in my home state of California. Simply put, home staging is a manner of presenting a home for sale so that it will appeal to the broadest buying audience, 'setting the stage' as it were, so that when the ready, willing and able buyer walks through the door, they are immediately hooked. There is nothing here that is dishonest in any way, and no trickery is involved. It is a simple technique that makes the most of what your home already has, thus allowing prospective buyers to see it in its most favourable light and – more importantly – to see themselves living there. Home staging enables a buyer to mentally 'move in' to your home.

I am often asked to define the most common mistake sellers make when trying to sell their homes. The answer is fairly simple: they assume that because they are comfortable in their own home and love it just the way it is, a prospective buyer will feel the same. Nothing could be further from the truth. Buyers need to be able to visualise themselves and their things in a home before even thinking of making an offer. They have to be able to see it as theirs, not yours. Which is not something that takes place purely by chance.

One would think that sooner or later the British viewing public would get wise to the notion that what I have been preaching works. You would think, moreover, that more and more people would be aware that proper presentation of their properties would not only lead to a quick sale, but also get a higher price. So why, then, are there still homes being put up for sale that are unkempt, cluttered, dirty and poorly presented? Well, the answer is simple. It's called denial.

Let me explain. You've heard me say that 'the home is the metaphor of the self'. This means that the state of one's inner self is reflected in the state of one's home. That is why clearing away clutter and reorganising belongings can effect a change in one's life. It allows a person to become 'unstuck' and able to move on. When I first visit a house, I must quickly determine why it has not sold. First I have a look at the space itself and define the problem areas. These are the familiar clutter, bold colours, shabby conditions and bad furniture placement. Then I determine the corrections that have to be made in order to set the property right. This is the easy part.

What might not be completely obvious is that I then need to determine the psychological issues surrounding the homeowners' situation that allow them to 'pretend' to be selling their homes, without ever actually achieving a sale. This is where things get somewhat more complicated. You see, even though people convince themselves consciously that they want to move, more often than not in these extreme cases, there are underlying issues that exist on a subconscious level that stand in their way. These are usually based on fear of change and are manifested in various scenarios. Here are some of the most common issues:

- Living in the past: The house holds memories – a family home where children have moved on, a once happy marriage that has collapsed, a spouse who has passed on.
- Loss of fortune: Due to unfortunate personal or financial circumstances, selling the house would mean a step down in terms of status.
- Punishment of a spouse or partner: The house needs to be sold as part of a divorce settlement or because of a job transfer, creating underlying resentment and resistance.
- Loss of control: These people can't bear rocking the boat. It would be too chaotic.
- Lack of support systems: This is common with those living on their own. They just can't seem to do it without help.
- Arrogance: These people think that their house is wonderful exactly the way it is and that anyone else who doesn't see it the same way is just ignorant.
- Fear: These people have no plan and so have nothing to look forward to.
- Greed: Their house is worth less than the figure they are asking for it.
- Laziness: People will come up with hundreds of excuses, none of which holds water.

You've seen such people on the programme. They surround themselves with clutter, dirt, unfinished DIY jobs and overgrown gardens. They make excuses such as lack of time or money; they blame others – their spouses, children, even their estate agents! And in so doing they never have to take that big scary step called moving. So while the House Doctor team goes about making changes to the house, I spend time helping these people see why their home hasn't sold. It is an amazing process to watch. As their home becomes decluttered and depersonalised, they begin to detach themselves from it. Often they get upset, even angry at first. This is a natural part of 'letting go'. Then gradually as they become more and more involved, they begin to wonder how they could have let things go for so long. Finally there comes a turning point when they actually see and appreciate the result of all our efforts. Although it looks a thousand times better, it no longer feels like their home. In fact, they feel slightly uncomfortable there. They have finally made the mental and emotional break. They are ready to sell. They begin talking about moving on in a positive manner, begin visualising their future. The House Doctor's task is complete.

THE THREE KEY INGREDIENTS:

- commitment
- detachment
- cooperation

Commitment: Unless someone is truly committed to selling their home and mentally and emotionally prepared to move on they will not take all the necessary steps along the path to getting it sold. Be clear on the result that you want to achieve before beginning what can be the stressful process of selling and moving house.

Detachment: You need to be able to step back and view your home through 'buyers' eyes', with your vision not clouded by personality, memories or emotion. This is the point at which I have to remind prospective sellers of this crucial mental nuance: 'You are not selling your home, you are selling a house.' An impersonal and objective attitude is necessary in order to achieve the desired result.

Cooperation: Unless there is the cooperation and involvement of all household members, the task at hand will be extremely daunting. Everyone involved needs to be 'on the same page' in order to make it work. It must be the case of all energies on board, moving towards the same goal – the sale.

It is a proven fact that buyers are willing to pay a higher price for a home that they feel they do not have to invest a lot of time and money into putting right. But they are not often able to see through your 'personality' to the home of their dreams. It is amazing how blind you can become to the things you live with day to day. Small things that you have grown accustomed to, like your

TOP 10 THINGS YOU SHOULD DO

1 **Neutralise:** Tone down your wall colours and floor colourings to provide a clean, blank canvas. Use stronger colours sparingly as accents to create a pleasing, well-thought-out scheme that runs throughout the house. The goal is to create a look that will appeal to the broadest buying audience.

2 **Depersonalise:** Get rid of family photos and children's drawings. Your buyer won't want to be distracted by your life. Let them concentrate on the rooms themselves.

3 **Declutter:** Tidy up EVERY room. Pack up and store or get rid of everything that you do not use on a regular basis. If a buyer can't even see a room, he is not going to be able to visualise himself living in it.

4 **Clean, clean, and clean again:** No one wants to live with another person's dirt, so clean like you've never cleaned before. And don't do it just once and then forget about it. Have a regular cleaning schedule involving all family members.

5 **Check your kerb appeal:** The look of the outside of your house is as important as the inside. It should immediately say to buyers, 'I'm a lovely house. Come inside', not, 'I'm not worth bothering with; keep driving.'

6 **Keep your pets under control:** Confine them to a specific area while you are selling your home. Many people find animal presence offensive and the smell off-putting. Why alienate them?

7 **Define each room or area:** Remember, you're selling a lifestyle so make sure your buyer is clear where he can comfortably entertain, dine, study or play.

8 **DIY now:** Finish off all those little jobs that can often signal that you may have left other, more important things unattended to as well.

9 **Ensure your lighting is sufficient:** If necessary, change bulbs to brighter ones or invest in some new light fittings.

10 **Accessorise:** Use mirrors wherever possible to maximise light and space. Dress your rooms with carefully chosen and coordinated accessories. Use colour to tie the room together. And don't forget plants, fresh flowers and pleasing fragrances, which appeal to the buyer's senses.

TOP 10 THINGS YOU SHOULD NEVER DO

1 **Carpet your bathroom:** Bathroom carpets do tend to hold moisture, often look drab and can smell. Use a water-resistant floor-covering instead.

2 **Paint the walls in garish colours:** However much you like bright colours, your buyer may find them overwhelming and they often make a room seem smaller and darker. To sell your house, paint walls in warm, neutral shades.

3 **Leave out the remains of yesterday's dinner party:** Nobody's interested in how good a cook you are or how many people you can entertain at once. Do the washing up the night before and make sure all scraps of evidence are put away before the estate agent calls.

4 **Leave the TV or blaring music on:** I sometimes hide the television altogether by putting it in a cupboard or behind a screen. Controllable noise provides an unnecessary distraction when you want people to concentrate on the room itself.

5 **Leave beds unmade or clothing strewn about:** No one wants to see your 'dirty laundry'.

6 **Believe other people will want to embrace your way of life:** When people look round your house they should be able to imagine themselves living there surrounded by their own things. Don't prevent that happening by leaving your own things, such as photos, travel souvenirs, mementoes, etc. on display.

7 **Raise red flags in the buyer's mind:** Don't leave anything that will make the buyer suspect there may be more trouble and expense than they can see. Does an unattended damp patch signal wet rot? Or a stained ceiling mean that the roof needs to be replaced?

8 **Block the views:** If the house has great views, make the most of them by clearing clutter from the window ledges, polishing the windows and putting up curtains.

9 **Have the house too warm or too cold:** A buyer needs to feel comfortable and relaxed while viewing your home, and not like he can't wait to escape.

10 **Engage in lengthy conversations with viewers:** Leave that to your estate agent. After all, isn't that why you hired him/her in the first place?

untidy garden, unfinished repairs, unnecessary clutter, dingy carpet or even your dog could be costing you money, or losing you that long-awaited sale.

I am not referring to some mysterious secret here. There's no complicated technique; rather, it is purely an issue of common sense. The key is to 'neutralise' your home – in effect, to take your personality out of the house so that buyers can imagine themselves as the one living there. You need to detach yourself from your home in order to be able to move on and achieve your dream. You are no longer living in your home, you are selling it, and these are two very different things. Harsh words, but if this concept seems strange to you at first, perhaps uncomfortable or even unnatural, it is nonetheless true. Remember, though, it is just a means to an end. You do want to move, don't you?

HOW DO YOU START?

The first and most difficult thing to do is to take a good look at your home critically and objectively through 'buyer's eyes'. How would a complete stranger who is interested in buying a house in your neighbourhood view your home? Remember, there is always the competition. Keeping this thought foremost in your mind, begin by standing across the street and imagine you are a prospective buyer driving by. Would you be interested in stopping to view your home? Does it compare well to the other houses on the street? Does its exterior make you want to go inside and see more? If not, then make a careful note of any possible improvements that would make your home more inviting. Kerb appeal is critical – after all, if the buyer doesn't make it to the front door, you will have lost him or her. There are no second chances.

Next, go inside. Pen and paper in hand, go carefully through each room noting anything that needs clearing, cleaning, mending or brightening. The most important rooms are the living room, main bedroom, kitchen and bathroom, so concentrate your efforts here if you have to choose. Be very tough on yourself. Remember you are seeing your home through a buyer's eyes. Buyers are very critical and they tend to focus on anything that might give them an excuse to make you a lower offer. Why give them the opportunity? Anything that could raise a possible objection in a buyer's eyes should be taken care of beforehand. This effort will mean money in the bank for you. Don't forget your garden and all other outside space. These are often neglected by home sellers and can sometimes make the difference between getting and losing a sale. Always bear in mind that buyers need to feel they are getting the most for their money.

Now that you have completed your list, go back through your house and make sure that you have left nothing out. If there is any question in your mind as to whether or not something should be done, do it. Trust me on this one. It will be worth it in the long run. Remember — no pain, no gain.

House doctoring is certainly a technique that can be learned, although it does help immensely to have a good design sense or 'eye'. In staging a home, the objective, as I've said before, is to eliminate as much of the owner's personality (family photos, knickknacks and mementoes, highly personalised decorating and/or colour statements) as possible. When I'm staging a home, I couldn't care less whether the client likes the result or not (as you may have seen in the series!).

Staging is an editing process. Everything personal, unnecessary, or extreme is removed from the home and replaced with things that have a neutral, minimal and harmonious feel to them (whereas interior design is a supplementing process; its goal is to surround the client with beautiful things that have a personal meaning to them as individuals). Staging is done with no one in particular in mind (or rather, with everyone in particular in mind) and in a staging project, no matter what the asking price of the home, the object is to spend as little money as possible to get the expected result. I try to use a lot of what the client already owns, arrange it differently, and spend money only on essentials, most of which the client can take with them when they move. I always reserve the last bit of cash for things like fresh flowers, cheery plants, fluffy new towels, colourful cushions, scented soaps and potpourri — those little extras that cost almost nothing, but give the impression of freshness and attention to detail. The entire environment is 'staged' to give positive subliminal suggestions to prospective buyers, in much the way as in the world of advertising.

In America we are used to having a lot more space. Therefore, on average our homes are bigger. They are also, overall, built far more recently. I'm not boasting, just making a comparison. Actually, this realisation has helped me to understand some of the difficulties that arise when applying my principles of house doctoring here in Britain. I have been faced with some real challenges and have tried in each instance to offer a more appropriate alternative.

We Americans also like to hide things. We put our TVs and audio equipment behind doors . Our rubbish bins are under the sink or at the back of our homes. Our washers, dryers and ironing boards are in the laundry room. How many homes have I seen in Britain where the telly has pride of place in the sitting room? The ironing board is there, too. After all, how can you possibly iron without watching telly, and why bother taking it down if you only have to put it back up again? More astounding to me are the rubbish bins in the front garden as well as prominently displayed in every room of the house.

Finally, this brings me to my number one pet peeve — clutter. You would think that with space at such a premium the logical reaction would be to eliminate any excess clutter. On the contrary — in Britain there is a whole culture of wanting to hang onto everything, 'just in case'. Perhaps it is a hark back to the poverty of the war years, or just a reticence to spend money. Whatever the reason may be, the result can be lethal when the time to sell comes.

Now you have the formula for success. The rest is up to you. My experience shows that if you use this technique to prepare your home for sale, your expenditure of time, money, and effort will not go unrewarded. Your house will sell quickly and for its highest and best price.

SPACE AND HOW TO CREATE IT

When selling your home, you must ensure that it looks as inviting and spacious as possible so that buyers can imagine themselves already comfortably installed. There are a number of ways of doing this that will cost you next to nothing, yet will contribute greatly to increasing the value of your home.

declutter

Begin by taking a good look around your home, starting with the outside. Are there any children's toys, bicycles, skates or shoes on view? How about old newspapers or piles of post? Overflowing rubbish bins, gardening tools, empty pots or pots filled with dying plants? If you can answer yes to three or more of these items, then you might have to hire a skip before going any further. If your excuse is that you haven't anywhere to store the items, but that these items are actually useful to you, invest in an inexpensive storage shed for the back of the house.

Now, step inside. Before you begin you will need a supply of sturdy storage boxes, bubble wrap or tissue paper and packing tape. Separate all your possessions into four categories: those you need on a daily basis, those you want to take with you to your new home, but don't have room for or any need to use at the moment, those you are finished with, but could be useful to someone else, and those that are rubbish. Each room's clutter will be different in nature, but with one common denominator: it is interfering with your objective of getting the highest and best price for your home. The entrance tends to be a dumping ground for hats and coats, umbrellas, shoes, shopping bags and the post. The sitting room and dining room will usually be cluttered with books, ornaments, CDs, stereo equipment, dead plants, old magazines and even children's toys. In the bedroom the biggest offender is the wardrobe. Not only could you most likely dump half your clothes without ever missing them (we wear 20% of our clothing 80% of the time), the wardrobe can also be a real catch-all for homeless items – old luggage, mementoes, shoes, etc. The kitchen is another story – cluttered work surfaces and cupboards full of mismatched dishes, food well past its 'sell-by' date, redundant appliances, empty bottles and cans. Children's rooms are a storehouse for outgrown toys, books, clothes, old school projects and collections of all sorts. And lastly, the bathroom – here the biggest offenders are unused cosmetics and cleaning products, as well as tatty linens.

Subject your entire house to a real blitzkrieg, and then go through a second time with a fine toothcomb. Pack everything you are not keeping into boxes. Get it off the premises NOW. Take some to the dump or the tip, some to the car boot sale or charity shop. What you are planning to keep can go straight into storage in a neat and organised fashion in the cellar, loft or shed. If necessary, temporarily rent a storage locker. You'll feel better immediately, lighter, as if you can breathe more easily. And you should do – you've just (without it costing an arm and a leg) added value to your home.

storage

Now that you have created space inside your cupboards to hold essential belongings, it may still be worth investing in additional storage items to tidy up your home. Clothes look terrible hung on an open rail so beg, buy or even make a wardrobe in which to keep them. Shoe tidies will keep shoes neatly hidden within your wardrobe. Hooks or racks can often be fitted on the backs of cupboard doors for extra storage, but take care not to overload them. Have toiletries in a bathroom cabinet rather than on an open shelf, or buy some pretty storage baskets. Simple boxes to hold blankets or children's toys can be made from MDF and can double as seats. TVs are better housed in a cabinet – see if you can add doors to an existing shelving unit. If a spare bedroom is doubling as an office, invest in a small sofa bed.

Look at any dead space you may have and consider whether it could be used for storage. Alcoves are ideal places to put up shelves or a low cupboard. What about under the stairs or below the eaves? When did you last look behind you as you walked into a room? The space round a doorway can be used for shelving or cupboards provided they don't block the passageway. How about installing some inexpensive shelving in your cellar or loft for those items you don't use that often?

define and divide space

Think of the basic needs all of us have in our lives — sleeping, eating, working, playing, relaxing, cleansing — and then make a point of creating a space for each of them within your home, even if it only takes up a corner. Just rearranging or thinning out the furniture in a room can often accomplish this, so that the focus of a particular area, such as the fireplace, becomes clear. I often find proper dining space is sorely neglected in this country. You may enjoy eating off your knees in front of the TV but, when selling your house, you must show the buyer that there is a more civilised alternative. This may mean setting up a part of your living room, kitchen or hall for dining for the purposes of the viewing, but, artfully arranged, it will add pounds to your pocket. Often homeowners have a forgotten or unused space, such as a small closet that could become a study, a rooftop that could be a lovely outdoor room, or a box room that could make a study, second bedroom or perhaps a kid's playroom. Similarly, the garden needs to be presented as a place for barbecuing, dining or recreation.

Sometimes it helps to divide space when attempting to define it. Divisions do not have to be solid or structural, but can give the impression of separating one area from another while retaining the sense of space – for example, a curtain or screen that can be removed to one side when required. Carefully arranged shelving or stacking cubes are very effective. Garden trellis can be used creatively indoors just as well as out. Furniture placement can force the flow of traffic through the space and can be used to divide a room as well.

colour

Cool colours, lighter values, and plain or minimal patterning cause walls and ceilings to recede and are best for creating a spacious feel. Dark or bright colours, or loudly patterned wallpapers or carpet, make a room claustrophobic. A few tricks will enhance the sense of space. If the ceilings are low, paint them almost white (add a touch of yellow, as ceilings tend to grey out in their own shadow) to visually raise them, or use vertically striped wallpaper. Avoid horizontal borders or divisions. If ceilings are too high, add a dado rail, or painted wallpaper border to the wall a couple of feet below the ceiling. Paint the ceiling and up to the border the same medium to deep tone. A disproportionately long room can be made to look shorter by painting the two end walls a deeper or warmer colour. Generally, the most spacious-seeming rooms have little pattern, pale walls and carpet, and use colour as accents in accessories, to prevent the room from looking too impersonal.

light

It is important that as much natural light as possible reaches the room so make sure the windows are clean and not blocked by curtains or objects positioned in front of them, either indoors or out. Be imaginative with your window dressing (see How to Dress Windows, page 70). Venetian or roller blinds can be used for privacy or to hide an unpleasant view, but will still admit light. Window coverings such as voile or muslin will allow a diffuse light to enter the room or you could use spray etch or frosted plastic film to obtain a similar effect. Re-glossing the woodwork in an off-white will help reflect more light into the room. (Paints with a slight sheen are more reflective than matt finishes.) Light will also be reflected from anything that is made of glass, metallic or crystal, and from smooth or shiny fabrics rather than those that are heavily textured. Reflected light also increases the proportions of a room so work out the optimum position to hang a mirror. Mirrors work well with artificial lighting too. If placed behind candles, above a fireplace, near a pendant light or even lit from behind, they will give the impression of adding more light and space.

Use artificial lighting to highlight various areas of a room to make it appear more spacious. And use uplighters and downlighters for different effects (see Tackle Lights and Switches, page 96).

furniture

Never has the phrase 'less is more' been more apt than when selling your home. Consider thinning out your furniture and even putting some of it into storage, if necessary. The amount of furniture in a room and its arrangement has a huge effect on the visual space and this needs to be given careful attention when selling. Every room must have a focal point. If one doesn't exist, you can create one by the arrangement of furniture. Chairs and sofas should never block the traffic flow through a room. Arranging furniture around the perimeter of the room makes the space look smaller. Pay attention to scale and balance. Make sure that the individual pieces are not too large for the room, and that furniture is equally distributed. And never, ever obscure an important feature in a room, such as a French window, alcove or fireplace with a piece of furniture; rather, arrange your furniture so that the feature becomes a focal point.

COLOUR SCHEMES

Colour is a very personal thing. Everybody brings their own associations to different shades, which is exactly why you shouldn't impose your taste on any potential buyer. A bright blue might remind you of your Australian holiday, but others may find it cold and uncheering. If you have a strong colour scheme in a room, try to tone the wall colour down so that it harmonises and becomes less obtrusive. This generally tends to make the room look bigger, too. Try the new colour out in at least three areas of the room so you can see how it looks in changing lights. However, if you're looking at a room with a total personality by-pass, it's not too late to establish a colour scheme by introducing coloured accessories. A confident combination of cushions and/or throws, rugs and carefully picked ornaments can introduce harmony and character. If you're unsure about which colour to use with another, consult the colour wheel (see opposite). Although you may favour energising bright colours from opposite sides, in this instance it would be wiser to use harmonising adjacent shades to create a calm and relaxing mood in the main rooms. Don't make the mistake of slapping on a coat of white paint as an easy solution. It can look bare and uncompromising and will subtly alter in shade, depending on the contents of the room and the light. Much better to go for soft neutrals and pastels that will blend with what's there, keeping the atmosphere without intruding on it.

- Oil-based gloss – hard-wearing, shiny finish for woodwork, indoor and out.
- Oil-based eggshell – matt finish for interior woodwork.
- Acrylic gloss and eggshell are water-based variants. They're quick to dry, but not quite as hard-wearing as their oil-based relations.
- Primers and undercoats – use a primer and undercoat on any bare wood before applying your top coats.
- Water-based emulsion, silk or matt – for interior walls and ceilings.
- Solid emulsion – quick , easy and clean to use. Comes in its own tray. Non-drip, so good for ceilings, but costs more than regular emulsion.
- Specialist paints – if painting radiators, tiles or floors, make sure you get the appropriate paint. Ordinary emulsion or gloss won't stay put.

SELL IT!

If the walls are bright, patterned or just plain ugly, paint them in light, neutral colours. The idea is to trick your potential buyers into visualising themselves living there. They just won't be able to do that if they're overwhelmed by the colour of the walls. Most people don't want to move into a house where they know they're immediately going to be involved in a heavy decorating job. If the background is neutral, then you can introduce splashes of colour with rugs, cushions, throws, table runners and flowers.

Above: The colour wheel is an extremely useful tool when it comes to choosing paints. If you choose colours from the same side of the spectrum, they will blend naturally together, creating a soothing and harmonious atmosphere. However, if you want to create a more vibrant effect, pick colours that are opposite each other, being careful to use different strengths of tone so they complement one another rather than cancel each other out.

CREATING AMBIENCE

Staging your house is first and foremost a marketing exercise. You have to make your home seem the most desirable property in the area. Your potential buyers must leave feeling certain that this is the only house for them. Of course presenting them with an attractive home that looks as if it can be moved into without any work being done to it is essential. But there are various subliminal suggestions that you can offer that will make the place seem even more attractive. The game is to play with your buyers' senses so that you hook them into feeling comfortable. Imagine how you can make a subtle appeal to each of the five senses: sight, hearing, taste, smell, touch. Each room should be looking its best – clean, tidy, but lived in. If it's the evening, remember to turn the lights on so rooms are at their most inviting. Arrange the lights to emphasise the best features. A decoratively laid table can offer a subliminal invitation to anyone who enters. Soft music could be playing in the background. Flowers and plants help clear the air and give a feeling of life. Most effective of all can be the addition of pleasant smells. After all, no one enjoys the smell of yesterday's cooking, damp washing, cigarette smoke or pets. Your buyer will only remember the general welcoming atmosphere of the house, not the individual tricks you have used to seduce them.

Above: Candles can be used to create instant atmosphere – they are soft, romantic and flattering.

SELL IT!
Be ruthless when it comes to dealing with your pets. It's easy to get used to their smell – so ask a friend to be brutally honest with you. Does your house smell? Your buyer won't want evidence of your child's pet hamsters or beloved cats and dog the moment they cross the threshold. All pets should be banished to the garage or to a willing friend while you are showing people round. Once you've got rid of any unwanted smells, tackle the problem of pet hairs. Brush and vacuum until you're sure they have all gone. Now your house is ready to show at its best.

Left: Getting your home ready to be viewed needs careful thought. Open the windows wide to let the fresh air in. Make sure that all your plants are well watered and healthy. Check that any half-burned candles are replaced with new ones. Replace any dead light bulbs, ensuring that they are the right wattage. The smell of coffee, even if from only one cup, can be enough to begin to seduce even the most hard-nosed buyer. Brightly coloured scatter cushions can be an eye-catching addition to any room, both brightening it up and giving the impression of relaxed comfort.

Eliminate any unpleasant smells by opening windows.

Scented candles, a drop or two of vanilla essence on a light bulb or a stick of cinnamon in a warm oven smell delicious.

Potpourri in the living room and a bowl of lemons in the dining room or kitchen look attractive and counter any odours.

The smells of baking bread and freshly brewed coffee are notoriously seductive when it comes to showing off your home.

Play soft music, but nothing that jars.

Healthy green-leaved plants refresh and contribute a sense of well-being.

Fresh flowers add colour and fragrance to a room.

USING ACCESSORIES

Once you've achieved that all-important neutral background, largely by eliminating bold colours and patterns, or too many contrasting colours on the walls of a room, it's time to look at the accessories you can use to build colour back in. Accessories can carry a colour theme through your house, pulling the look of each room together. You must ruthlessly remove all the expendable bits and pieces and only replace with things that are essential to the look. Check in the back of your cupboards. I've seen forgotten wedding gifts come into their own at this moment. If you are really stuck, it's time for a bit of

retail therapy – after all anything you buy will go with you to your new home. Go easy though, you don't want to confuse your buyer into thinking they've walked into a bazaar. Cushions, throws and ornaments may brighten up a living room in moderation, while fluffy towels, new soaps and a shower curtain can transform a bathroom. You may want to colour-coordinate a few items on the kitchen worktop – matching kettle, toaster and jars for tea, coffee and sugar can jolly things up. New candles look good in almost every room and, of course, candlesticks can reflect the style of the house, traditional or modern, and be used to introduce colour, too. Use large pictures or a mirror on a blank wall. Accessories make the difference between a bland, uninteresting house and a vital, desirable home.

Right: The look of a room can be pulled together by coordinating the curtains and cushions, or throws and cushions.

- Clear all clutter.
- Choose the colour scheme you want to develop.
- Rediscover what there is in the house and use things in a different way.
- Shop for a few essentials that will pull the look of a room together.
- Tread a fine line between unlived-in and overcrowded.
- Replace worn accessories such as towels, tea towels and bits of soap.
- Replace tired or torn lampshades to colour-match the room.

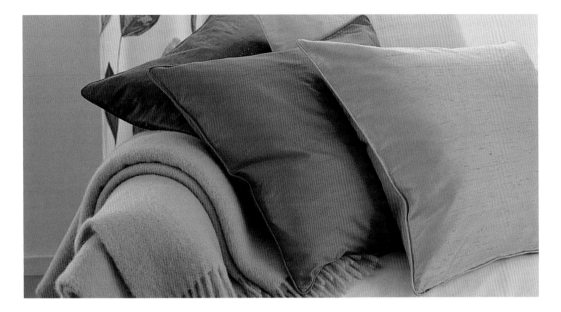

Above: Colourful cushions and throws make the perfect finishing touch and can transform the appearance of a room.

Left: Don't underestimate the effect of fluffy new towels and bathmats. They add colour and a welcome touch of luxury. Check that you've thrown away all those unfinished old bits of soap and buy some beautifully scented replacements.

SELL IT!

The first and most essential rule for every home staging is to clear the clutter. Mess all too easily becomes familiar junk that we are used to having around. But it gives the wrong impression of a room. It makes it look smaller and sends unhelpful messages to your buyers. You must make it as easy as possible for them to imagine themselves living here with their things. Tidy away family photos and books. If you can't find space to store the less personal stuff, throw it in the boot of your car and take as much as possible to the nearest dump.

EXTERIORS & HALLS

The first sight any prospective purchaser has of your property is the outside – the view from the road and the entrance door. Is your front garden a bit neglected? Don't allow this space to let down the appearance of your house. And remember, a back garden can be a huge asset when selling a house, but it's a space that's easy to overlook.

Signalling the way in to your home is important and making the front door stand out is one way to do it. Paint it a striking colour and it will immediately add interest to the front of the house.

It's vital to properly present your hallway. It's where potential buyers make the transition from the outside world into your home, often making up their minds about it within minutes of walking through the front door. And so it's vital to make sure those first impressions are the best.

EXTERIORS

When selling your house, one of the most important things to consider is how it looks from the outside. First impressions are often what make or break a sale. It's not much use having a perfect designer-style interior if the outside of the building is so scruffy that prospective buyers drive right past.

Stand across the road from your house and take a good long look. Can you put your hand on your heart and say that its appearance can't be improved? What about the paintwork? Is it in reasonably good repair? It may be worth having it redone. Is it perfectly clear where your property begins and the neighbours' ends? Are there any DIY jobs that need doing?

Look at the front garden – tidy up and replace any dead plants in window boxes so that you have a welcoming display instead.

TOP 10 TIPS

1 Define your boundaries. Buyers need to know exactly what they are getting for their money, so if necessary, invest in some new fencing.

2 Mow the grass, weed the flowerbeds and purchase some flowering border plants to give life and colour to the dingiest garden.

3 Make sure you have adequate lighting, in front and at the back of your home.

4 Don't forget about how your house looks when viewed from the garden – paint exterior walls a bright welcoming colour.

5 Turf over your children's football pitch and keep them off it until the house is sold.

6 Make an area where you can put a garden table and chairs. Immediately it transforms a garden or conservatory into another area that can be enjoyed in the sun.

7 Paint your front and back doors and polish all the door furniture so it gleams. It immediately suggests you take as much care of the inside. Be sure that your house numbers are easily visible.

8 Put a container or two of flowers, or a hanging basket, as a welcome by the front and back door.

9 Add an interesting water feature, an attractive garden light, or even some garden sculpture as a finishing touch.

10 Have a regular weekly maintenance programme to keep the outside of your home looking great throughout the whole marketing period.

No matter how small your back garden may be, you must make the most of it. It represents cash in your pocket – it's as simple as that: providing an extra outdoor room will add value to your house. You may have been meaning to clear the jungle for months. Now's the time to do it. Tidy up existing plants and brighten things up with some border plants from the garden centre. If necessary, lay new turf – your buyer wants a garden, not a football pitch. Your buyers will relish the idea of being able to sit outside in the summer enjoying the fruits of your labours and adding some of their own.

Check your paths – flagstones can begin to look green and slippery if they're not religiously cared for. For a completely different, more informal look, cover them with white gravel. It is an inexpensive treatment that can easily be changed ,but it gives new life and light to the garden.

Always remember that, when in the garden, your buyer will notice the back of the house, so carry out the same checks as you did for the front. Painting the back door and standing a potted plant beside it will make it look cheerful and welcoming.

Finally, improve the approach to the front door, perhaps by lining the front steps or a short path with a few potted plants, which will lead a visitor in. Remember, a buyer usually makes a decision to buy within the first thirty seconds of entering a home, so make sure that a potential buyer enters your house in a positive frame of mind.

REVAMP YOUR EXTERIOR FOR...

Creating a good first impression is vital, so it's worth spending as much as you can afford on the front-of-house appearance. Invest in some paint, perhaps some new fencing and a few plant pots or window boxes. Replace any cracked or broken tiles on the garden path, and if the front door furniture is past its prime replace with a new letterbox, knocker and handle.

Under £50		Under £100		Under £200	
Paint front door	£10	Paint front door	£10	Paint front door	£10
Replace door furniture	£20	Replace door furniture	£20	Replace door furniture	£20
Buy new plants	£15	Buy new plants	£15	Buy new plants	£15
		Buy new fencing	£50	Buy new fencing	£50
				Paint exterior walls	£20
				Buy garden furniture	£80

Give it kerb appeal

Has your house got kerb appeal? If it hasn't and you want a quick sale, it's time to address the problems. Buyers must be made to want to come into your house and not drive straight past it. A messy exterior throws up a red flag to them. After all, if you don't pay attention to the outside of the house, what's the inside going to be like?

DIAGNOSIS

The unpainted dingy rendering and peeling front door didn't do much for this house's kerb appeal. Nor did the dirty, bare windows on the first floor; there's nothing more depressing than staring through layers of grime. The plants needed sorting out, too – this was meant to be the front garden of a town house, not a nature reserve – and a lot of weeding was required.

CURE

Whitewashing the rendering and painting the front door a new glossy colour gave the house a lift and made it stand out from its surroundings. After cleaning the windows, we then hung clean curtains at the upstairs windows to tie in the look of the exterior. Finally, some careful planting and judicious pruning in the front garden made the whole thing look more managed. The impression of care and time spent will influence a buyer's perception of the inside of the house, too.

Define the area

It's important that the boundaries of your property are clear — a buyer wants to know exactly what he or she is looking at, and what land is and isn't yours. To this end, you may want to invest in some fencing, a brick wall or hedging plants. Weed overgrown paths and emphasise any areas such as parking spaces.

DIAGNOSIS

It's as important to define the external areas of the house as it is the interior ones. Nobody in their right mind would have wanted to get further than the front door of this house. The car parking area was unfinished and made the path to the door muddy and unattractive. Building work had been left incomplete, with ugly piles of rubble heaped up outside.

CURE

Once we'd cleaned up the mess that should have been the front garden we decided to separate the path from the parking area with a low wall. The wall was built from stock that matched the house and so it didn't detract from the general appearance of the house, but made a definite statement, emphasising the way to the front door. We chose white paint for the windows, and spruced up the front door with a fresh coat of paint, making it the focal point of the exterior. This simple tactic made the house look fresh and inviting.

Clean up

Give the outside a makeover. Mow the lawn, tidy the edges and invest in some attractive bedding plants to pretty borders up, or at least tidy the plants that are there. If it's autumn, sweep up the dead leaves. Clear away the children's tricycles and get rid of anything doggy. Take down the washing line and make sure that any rubbish that is long overdue for the dump is finally taken there.

DIAGNOSIS

This yard was suffering from terrible neglect. There was a dirty old barbecue out there, but it was hardly an inviting prospect. In addition, the sparsely planted flowerbed, a few empty plant pots and a discarded children's sandpit were not an attractive sight. The paintwork was looking very tired, too. I had to transform this yard into somewhere alive and welcoming.

CURE

It's always possible to jazz up a dead space by adding colour. In this case we concentrated on the green of the plants and any other colour would come from their flowers. We chose plants in a range of heights and foliage so we could create something consistently interesting to look at. We cleaned up the barbecue and got rid of the rubbish. However, had the budget allowed, we could have been a little more experimental, painting the door a strong colour and maybe even one of the walls as well, to add interest.

Paint it

An inexpensive coat of paint can transform the appearance of your exterior walls and fences. Pebble-dashed or rendered walls, in particular, will often benefit from being repainted. Another way of adding colour to a garden is to paint one of the walls a cheerful colour and add some hanging baskets.

DIAGNOSIS

This pebbledash was painted an extremely off-putting pink, which I felt was a huge strike against the property. The large paved area at the rear of the house was scruffy and uninviting, a shame when it should be presented as a positive bonus. The exterior of this house immediately cried out 'old-fashioned and neglected'; something had to be done.

CURE

I decided to blow a large part of the budget in repainting the exterior of this house, changing the ugly pink to a more sophisticated cream. And it worked. The house looked larger, more elegant and as if the owners still cared for it. The paved patio was the ideal space for sitting out and enjoying the sun. We turned it into another room with the simple addition of a garden table and chairs and it was obvious what pleasures this garden had in store. The addition of some flowering plants cheered things up no end.

Windows

Clean windows make a huge difference to the appearance of a house —
make sure they sparkle, inside and out. Clear all window sills of leaves
and, if they are large enough, you might want to add a colourful window
box. Peeling paint or broken sills won't impress anyone, so tidy up any
shabby bits of window frame and give them a lick of paint. Ensure that the
windows don't stick when opened, and never leave in any glass panes that
are cracked — get them professionally replaced. If you have any louvre
windows, you might want to replace them with fixed glass. Make sure all
curtains, blinds and shutters are clean and that they are evenly drawn
and hanging properly. If you have trees in the front garden, ask yourself
whether they need pruning. You don't want the trees to block the view of
the house and, most importantly, they shouldn't block the light coming
into the house.

WINDOWS

If any of your windows are beyond repair you should replace them. It may seem a big job, but it will make a difference to your sale. Whatever you do, make sure that the replacements are as close to the originals as possible. However, it is more likely that what you will be faced with are some minor repairs. All the paintwork should be touched up where necessary and washed where not. On the exterior of the house, it is safest to go for clean white gloss on the window frames, making sure that all the windows open and close properly. They can be decorated by using window boxes, provided they are well-planted and colourful. Make sure any curtains or blinds you can see from outside are clean and properly hung.

Above: Plastic-coated aluminium frames need to be carefully cleaned and, if necessary, repaired. Blinds should be straight and evenly displayed.

When staging a house, it's important to look outside 'the box', too. If there is a particularly good view then draw attention to it by dressing the appropriate window. Curtains don't need to be expensive or elaborate to be effective and they can add colour to the room. Make sure they blend with the general scheme and draw back to let in as much light as possible. Try not to hide the shape of an unusual and attractively designed window. Shabby old net curtains are one of my pet hates. If you want to retain privacy and light, the best solution is to invest in blinds. Venetian blinds are one effective choice, but roman blinds can be made in fine cotton or voile, which are more feminine and play the same trick. If the view's dire, you might want a curtain that covers the bottom half of the window only.

- Clean all windows until they sparkle.
- Wash the paintwork round them.
- Ensure that they all open and shut properly.
- Check that all window furniture matches and works.
- Investigate the different kinds of blinds on the market.
- Don't block the flow of sunlight into the room.

Top left: Leaded glass should always be clean to allow maximum possible light.

Top right: Stained or patterned glass can be a cheap, effective way of beautifying an entrance.

Above: You may want to lighten a dark hall, but remember that, if the solution is as extreme as this, you must keep the inside extremely tidy.

SELL IT!

Remember all those little jobs round the house that you've always meant to finish? Now's the time to do it. If you realise that the reason for the delay is because you don't really know what you're doing, then get someone in who does. It won't be expensive and it's vital to selling your house. Broken window catches, a front door bell that doesn't work or half-finished shelves convey an air of neglect and signal to a potential buyer that there may be other, more significant aspects of the house that have been left undone.

Design

Simplify the exterior of your property and consider the design of your garden. Is it a restful and inviting place to be? No? Then declutter and consider paving or decking in place of a constantly overgrown lawn. Create a focal point and screen off bins and sheds. If your garden is tiny put a mirror on a blank wall — it will make the garden seem much bigger.

DIAGNOSIS

This small garden was too busy. Everything jostled for attention and the hotchpotch flooring made it look even smaller. Too many things in a small space make it look claustrophobic. What it needed was a strong but simple design that would pull it into one coherent look, doing justice to, and maximising, the space available.

CURE

An impressive-looking solution to this patio was decking. Surprisingly inexpensive, it can be quick and easy to put down with immediate and stylish results. A stretch of trellising doesn't have to be throttled by climbing plants to be effective. Here, it provided additional height to the wall, further defining the boundary, but without interrupting the light falling on the garden. The keynote of the new garden was simplicity. The garden bench and table add a note of elegant sophistication, emphasised by the sparing choice of pot plants.

Planting

Dead plants and even just uncared-for plants add nothing whatsoever to the appearance of a garden. Empty flowerpots look forlorn and depressing. Go down to your local garden centre and ask their advice about the sort of plants that would grow happily in your patch — inexpensive bedding plants will invigorate the dreariest plot for at least as long as it takes to sell it. Even in winter, flowering plants can be bought to cheer up a neglected outdoor space. Then, suitably armed, return home, throw away the unhealthy specimens and design a simple planting plan. Paint flowerpots, pot a suitably large plant and use as a feature, and grow some sweet-smelling herbs. Repair any broken walls or fencing. If you're fortunate enough not to have had to re-turf, then mow your lawn and trim the edge. A proprietary weed killer should clear up the gaps between the patio flagstones and any garden path.

If you have trees, they might look more charming if they were pruned (again, depending on the time of year) and you should certainly remove any windfalls and fallen leaves in the autumn.

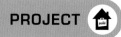# PLANT POTS

Use your imagination to create attractive plant containers that will brighten up the forgotten areas of your garden.

old bucket

What you need

- bucket
- drill
- hammer and nail
- polystyrene pieces
- plastic sheeting
- potting compost
- plants (see below)

ONE Take an old bucket and drill some drainage holes in its base. Alternatively, turn the bucket upside down and hammer a nail through the bottom to make several holes.

TWO To reduce the depth of the bucket, put in a layer of polystyrene pieces and cover with a sheet of plastic pierced with holes.

THREE Top up with compost then plant. This arrangement used pale apricot nicotiana, verbena, lilac lobelia and helichrysum for a light summery effect.

using compost and fertilisers

Garden soil can be used in plant containers, but it can bring pests, weeds and disease with it. It is better to use a proprietary brand of potting compost. To encourage growth, remember to water regularly so that the compost never dries out and use slow-release fertiliser capsules.

bicycle basket

ONE An old bicycle basket can make a great outdoor container for plants. It can be just as easily hung up, stood on a windowsill or attached to a wall through the hole in its back.

TWO Line the basket with hessian, a ready-made liner, or plastic with holes punched into it for drainage.

THREE Fill with compost then plant. This arrangement used a mix of sky-blue *Convolvulus sabatius*, pale mauve trailing petunia, and a selection of miniature pelargoniums. Together they create a wild, old-fashioned look that tones well with their country setting.

finding and using other types of containers

Look around the house and in junk shops for other items that could be given a new lease of life in your garden. Old, coloured enamel colanders, wire baskets, kettles or butler's sinks are just some of the things that can make plant containers. Add drainage holes where necessary or line with holed plastic so the compost stays in place. Wire baskets look best with an outer lining of moss disguising the plastic lining. Choose plants to complement or contrast with their surroundings.

Garden furniture

When selling your house, you should make the most of every asset it has. Outdoor space is a big plus, particularly for a town house, so never overlook a roof terrace. There's always room to create some space for sitting, or even eating, outside and there's a huge range of garden furniture available now in many different styles.

DIAGNOSIS

This roof terrace looked unloved and ignored. The owners had dumped rusty bicycle frames, dead plants and anything else they didn't want out there. We had to clear away the mess and we could then start to add a few finishing touches to put things right and make the terrace an inviting place.

CURE

Once we'd cleared the area of all the discarded rubbish, we added a smart set of garden table and chairs, which immediately gave purpose to the patio. There are so many different styles to choose from these days that you need to think carefully about the overall look you want to achieve and investigate the range of furniture available before buying. The wooden furniture we chose for this terrace has a simple rustic appeal that suits the space it inhabits. Some freshly potted plants completed the look and turned it into an inviting space.

Finishing touches

A judiciously placed table and a couple of chairs will always draw people into the garden on a sunny day. They will be able to imagine themselves entertaining friends or dining al fresco. Garden or patio furniture is easy to find at your local garden centre, nearby department store or DIY centre. The upside is that you can, of course, take it with you when you move. Or, if you're handy with a saw, why not make your own table, planter boxes or wood sculptures?

If you have an unattractive wall, cover it with cane screening or paint it. And, for or a real finishing touch, how about a fountain or water feature? It creates the feeling of serenity everyone wants from their outdoor 'sanctuary' and can help disguise traffic noise. Make an area where it will be pleasant to sit out and entertain.

FRONT DOORS & HALLS

Stepping through your front door into the entrance hall will create a lasting impression on your potential buyer. A smart front door will invite a good reaction, while the hall sets the mood for the rest of the house. If the hall is cluttered now's the time to clear it – tripping over shoes, bicycles and umbrellas won't endear the house to potential buyers.

Check the hall carpet and, if it is particularly shabby, replace it. To economise, you could use an offcut or consider sanding and varnishing your floorboards instead.

If you can't get rid of ugly features, then disguise them. A radiator looks better boxed in and the ledge provides a more useful place for letters than the floor. Your burglar alarm may prompt the buyer to question whether the house is burgled regularly. Move it to a more discreet position if you possibly can.

TOP 10 TIPS

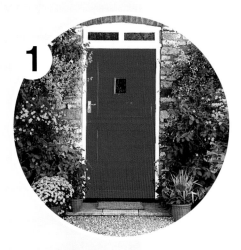

1 A fresh green plant or vase of flowers strategically placed at your front door adds a bit of life as well as a welcoming touch.

2 If you have a burglar alarm, box it in or relocate it, so it's not the first thing anyone notices on entering the house.

3 Remove all clutter so the passage into the house isn't restricted and the door opens freely.

4 Repaint dark, claustrophobic halls with a warm, paler colour to maximise the existing space and light.

5 Open up narrow hallway spaces by maximising both artificial and natural light, and ensuring nothing blocks the route.

6 If the floor covering shows signs of wear, get rid of it. Can you use the floorboards or tiles underneath? If not, recarpet.

7 Be sure that the lighting (both natural and artificial) is sufficiently bright, but not glaring. Update, if necessary.

8 Create a focal point by boxing in a radiator and using the shelf for a couple of favourite ornaments. This will break up the longest hallway.

9 Don't crowd the walls with pictures. It will make them close in. A couple of well-chosen ones is usually enough.

10 The stairs should lead invitingly upstairs, so consider whether it's worth investing in a new stair carpet. Replace missing banisters and, if necessary, smarten them all up with a lick of paint.

Don't crowd your walls with pictures; they will make the walls seem to close in. Hanging one or two carefully will do the trick and provides a welcoming touch. And if you have a hall that's no more than a narrow corridor, create a focal point by spotlighting one of the pictures or by using a vase of flowers on a small table.

Lighting is important. There's nothing worse than arriving somewhere that seems dingy and uncared for. Obviously you're not going to be able to create a new window, but you can clean the one that is already there, maximising the available light. Otherwise, look at the electrics. Would the atmosphere benefit from the addition of a new lightshade that's in keeping with the period of the house? Might it be worthwhile replacing that central spot with a simple tracking system that will throw light on the walls, again creating the illusion of space and taking the attention towards the rooms on either side? Most important of all, replace any dud bulbs with others of the right wattage.

Once you've ensured that the entrance to your house is a warm and inviting place, it's time to look at the rooms themselves.

REVAMP YOUR HALL FOR...

Lighting is important in a hall so, if necessary, invest in new light fittings, a lighter shade of wallpaper or paint, and new flooring. Consider boxing in a radiator, or adding a shelf, and do check the stairs – replace any missing banisters. Finally, a mirror will add to the impression of light and space.

Under £50		Under £100		Under £200	
Paint walls and woodwork	£20	Paint walls and woodwork	£20	Paint walls and woodwork	£20
Replace light fittings	£25	Replace light fittings	£25	Replace light fittings	£25
		Buy mirror	£40	Buy mirror	£40
				Recarpet or sand floor	£70
				Box in radiator and burglar alarm	£25

First impressions

A clean and inviting front door should open onto a hall that's uncluttered and bright, and that makes the visitor feel like exploring the rest of the house. Walking in from the street to a shabby carpet is a turn-off, as is scuffed and dirty paintwork, while bold, swirling wallpaper patterns will only make a hallway seem smaller.

BEFORE

AFTER

The first striking thing about this hall was its lack of period feel and the second was the colours that brought the walls inwards, minimising the space. Once I'd got rid of the horses adorning the wall and the intrusive side table, we could start. I nervously ordered the flat modern façades to be removed from the doors. Sure enough, behind them were the original panelled doors in good enough condition to need only a little restoration. Once they'd been sanded down, filled, had some beading added and been painted, they looked as good as new. Then it was the turn of the walls.

The vinyl wallpaper and pattern borders were stripped off to make way for some stick-on, paintable wood-panelling. This was extremely easy to fit, needing tacking only where we felt it needed the extra hold. Once the dado rail had been fitted and the walls and woodwork painted, the hall was beginning to take shape. The modern radiator, one of my pet hates, was an anachronism but a necessity so the best we could do was box it in. I wanted to add a little warmth by picking up the red from the runner and hanging a curtain in the same shade at the end of the corridor. The final key to the transformation was replacing the green carpet with one in a cool neutral shade. Now there was an entrance in keeping with the fine exterior of the house.

DOORS

A door can be a strong focal point. It is the architectural feature that introduces you to the space behind it and gives the first clue to what you might find there. Make a feature of your front door. If it is painted the same colour as the windows, it will lose impact. Much better to choose a strong colour, matching the frame with the window frames. Bear in mind the colour of your neighbours' doors, too – clashing colours can look awful. Painting your door doesn't cost much and can lift the appearance of the exterior of your house.

Apart from dividing one room from another and maintaining privacy between those spaces, doors can also be decorative. They can break up the monotony of a wall. Would your door look better if the frame or the panels were a different colour? Alternatively, if the walls are busy, you might want the door to blend into the background by painting it the same colour as the wall or extending bookshelves to run over the top of it. Don't block doors with pieces of furniture. It's important that the flow of the home is efficient, making any newcomer feel more comfortable there. Ask yourself if all the doors are absolutely essential. An archway may be as effective. Consider a tie-back curtain on an iron rod – it can be both elegant and space-saving. Or you might replace door panels with glazing. You'd be surprised how a dingy hallway can be made lighter and much less claustrophobic, even if you use etched, smoked or coloured glass.

Left: A sheer curtain covering a doorway into a dark hallway can both lighten the hall and keep the kitchen area separate.

Check that the style of your doors suits the period of your house.

All door furniture should match and be polished thoroughly.

Replace fittings with the simplest style if you're uncertain.

Make sure everything about the door works – hinges, bell, handle etc.

Decorate interior doors – contrasting panels and beading; stencilling on the frame or panels.

Don't block doors with furniture or clutter.

If a door isn't essential, remove it and make an archway, eradicating all signs of the hinges, which are easy to forget.

SELL IT!

Make sure all entrances are uncluttered, warm and welcoming. Mark the path to your front door with potted plants on either side. Or you may want to flank a door or french windows with single plant pots or hanging baskets.

Make sure the doors open properly and aren't hampered by a row of coats or muddy boots behind. Check that furniture doesn't stop any of the internal doors from opening or shutting properly. Draughts and a sense of everything being squashed into a room won't hasten your chances of a sale.

Far left: A small window in a front door can make a difference to a dark hallway.

Left: Door fittings that match gleam in welcome on this traditional panelled front door.

Above left : Ensure your doors match the period of your home and give them a kiss of life with a new coat of paint.

Above right : If a door is constantly left open, it may make sense to remove it altogether and create a feature of the resulting archway.

Decoration

Your hall should appear as light and welcoming as possible. If the walls are painted a strong colour, they will give the illusion of a smaller space. Open it up by painting a fresh neutral colour that leads effortlessly into the rooms beyond. Make sure the doors and frames are all painted the same colour. Strongly patterned wallpaper can also be overpowering so consider painting over it.

DIAGNOSIS

This hall, with its stark yellow and blue colour scheme, reminded me of nothing more than a doctor's waiting room. The effect was cold and impersonal and depressingly dark. The owners' choice of colours was off-puttingly dated and they had put no thought into making their hall an inviting transition point between the outside world and where they lived.

CURE

The first job was to repaint the hall. The yellow and blue was far from welcoming and much too overbearing for most people's taste. Instead, we chose a honey-tinted neutral for the walls, which immediately opened up the space. The blue coving, skirtings and door frames were transformed by being painted with a white gloss. And we said goodbye to the yellow gloss doors, which also succumbed to the power of the paintbrush. We left the yellow shades and used brown, beige and gold as accent colours. The hall looked much better.

DIAGNOSIS

This was a terrible entrance. The clashing wall colours made the space seem much more cramped than it really was. Dark and powerful colours tend to impose themselves on a space, making it smaller, whereas paler shades tend to make the walls recede. In a long, tall corridor it was essential to maximise the space available, at the same time inviting the eye towards the end.

CURE

We painted the overwhelming colours of the walls in a soft neutral shade with white gloss on all the woodwork, including the louvre doors. Apart from making the space look brighter, cleaner and twice the size, this also unified the look. We boxed in the storage heater and hung a picture and, of course, a mirror to help things seem lighter and airier. Barring the door to the kitchen with a child's safety gate gave a distinctly unwelcoming subliminal message, so we removed it. A good vacuuming and the hall was ready for viewing.

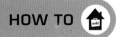

PAINT INTERIORS

Painting a room can transform its character, but make sure you choose the right finish to give the results you want.

which colour and finish?

The colour you choose can make a huge difference to the perception of a room. Pale colours make the walls and ceiling seem to recede, and the space seems bigger and airier. The shiny finishes of gloss, eggshell and vinyl silk reflect light to make a room look even larger, while a monochrome colour scheme — off-whites, beiges and taupes — will make it seem larger still. Dark colours close the walls in, making the space more intimate. Matt finishes will make it seem smaller, too.

If the room is too tall, make the ceiling seem lower by painting it a darker colour than the walls. The illusion of lowering it further can be achieved by extending the darker ceiling colour onto the upper portion of the wall. Mark the start point with masking tape in order to get a straight, clean dividing line. How far down the wall you paint is a matter of choice. It might be only as far as a picture rail or, in the absence of one, it may be the top quarter of the wall.

If your room seems too squat, get rid of all horizontal lines such as picture rails, borders or dados and paint vertical stripes on the walls. Even the most subtle differentiation between stripes will be enough to make the room grow. Painting the ceiling a pale colour will make it seem higher.

Remember that colour can profoundly influence mood, so it is important to select the right palette for the feeling you want and to choose the proportions well. White is clean, calming and peaceful. Red has connotations with passion. Blue can seem cool, while yellow is viewed as a sunny, upbeat colour. Selling your house demands the choice of soft neutrals precisely so they do not intrude into a buyer's consciousness, unduly distracting or unsettling him or her.

When choosing colours, take into account what furnishings are in the room. Tiny squares of colour on paint charts are not representative of what the colour will look like on all four walls. If possible, paint a large piece of lining paper or MDF and move it around the room so you can see exactly how it looks in different lights at different times of the day. In the cold English light, for example, it is often better to use slightly warmer colours to bring the room to life — off-white or cream is often better than pure white, while soft aquamarines, eau de nil, peaches and apricots are better than bright blues or oranges. Also look at the proposed colour during different times of the day and under artificial light. Think about when the room is used most often and judge whether or not this is when the colour looks its best.

preparation

Make sure all odd jobs are completed before painting. Fixing a sash cord or broken door or light switch later will mess up your finished paintwork. Remove furniture or stack it in the centre and cover with a dustsheet. Ensure the surfaces to be painted are clean and carefully prepared, repairing any damage such as blisters, flaking paint, chips and cracks.

technique

Get the right amount of paint on your brush by dipping it into the paint until one-third of the bristles are covered, then pressing it against the paint container. If using a roller, push it backwards and forwards in the paint tray, then up the slope of the tray to get rid of the excess paint. As you work, make sure the paint is 'laid off', or smoothed over, while wet. Remember, two thin coats of paint are better than one thick one. The order to paint a room is ceiling, walls, then woodwork.

painting techniques

Be sure to open windows and have adequate ventilation while avoiding drafts straight onto the paint itself.

Ceiling: If using a brush, begin in a corner near the window then work in strips away from the light. If using a roller, paint the corners the roller cannot reach with a small brush then cover the main area with alternating diagonal strokes.

Woodwork: For a flat-surfaced door, paint from top to bottom in strips, making sure you work fast enough to prevent the paint hardening before the section next to it hardens. For a panelled door, paint the panels first, working from each side to meet in the middle. Then paint the sections between them before finishing off with the top, bottom then sides of the door.

Windows: Apply masking tape to the edges of windows and begin painting the sections nearest the glass, working outwards to paint the window frame last. Pull the top of a sash window down and the bottom up before painting. Paint the meeting rail first then as much as possible of the bottom window and the top. Paint inside the top of the frame and 50cm (20in) down the outside runners. Almost close the window and paint the top 50cm (20in) of the inside runners and finish in the same order as the sash window.

Walls: Start at the top corner, work in strips down to the skirting board, then return to the top. Use a smaller brush to 'cut in' around the doors and windows. A roller should be used in alternating diagonal strokes so that gaps and joining lines are merged. Try to paint a wall while working in the same light so that you can see where you have covered. Make sure that you complete a wall before knocking off for the night, otherwise the line where you stopped then restarted will be noticeable.

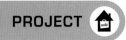
GILDED MIRROR FRAME

Mix metallic gold leaf and a bold coloured paint to give a fabulous finish to an old frame.

What you need

- old wooden frame
- medium-grade sandpaper
- small paintbrushes
- deep red acrylic stencil paint
- gold size (from art shop)
- talcum powder
- Dutch metal leaf (from art shop)
- scissors and ruler
- wrapping paper
- mirror glass (cut to fit)

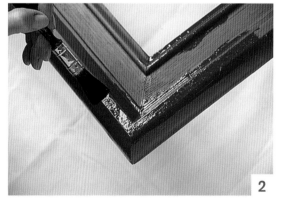

ONES and the frame and wipe it clean. Paint it with acrylic stencil paint, brushing along the grain of the wood. Leave to dry.

TWO Working over a small area at a time, brush gold size over the edges of the frame, omitting the central recess. Leave for about 10 minutes to allow the size to become tacky. Dust your fingers with talcum powder so the gold leaf will not stick to them.

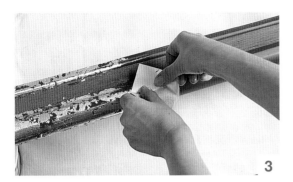

THREE Place a sheet of gold leaf, silver side down, on the size. Smooth it on then peel off the backing paper. Brush size onto the next section and smooth on more gold leaf, just overlapping it with the last. The patchy effect gives an aged look.

FOUR Cut four strips of wrapping paper to fit the frame's recess. Be sure to mitre the corners precisely so that they match exactly.

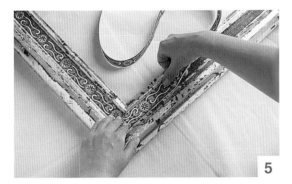

FIVE Brush gold size along the recess and stick the strips of wrapping paper in place, carefully lining up the mitred corners. Hide the joins by covering them with a motif cut out from the wrapping paper. Mount the mirror glass in the frame.

Stairs

The staircase from *Psycho* is not much of an invitation, so make sure there's a welcoming light at the top. If the stairs are narrow and steep, create a different illusion by lightening the wall colour and replacing the carpet with a paler shade. Check that the carpet is securely fixed and that any handrail is firmly secured to the wall. If the treads are in good condition, it may be more effective to use a runner than a fitted carpet. Replace and paint any missing banisters — it makes a world of difference. If you've got a slatted, banister-free staircase, then it's vital to create the illusion of something more secure. It's quite easy and inexpensive to add a banister up one side, if not both.

DIAGNOSIS

The owners had lived in this house for twenty years and I'm afraid it showed. The overall impression was of a dark and unfriendly space, with the busy carpet and general clutter making it seem tight and claustrophobic. The stairs looked menacing rather than inviting and both hall and stairway needed to feel lighter, more modern and far more appealing.

CURE

After removing the clutter, it was a simple matter of replacing the carpet with another in an acceptable neutral shade that was easier on the eye and looked much more contemporary. Running the same carpet through the hall and up the stairs can really bring a space together. I chose a soft yellow for the walls so that the space looked larger. Painting the ceiling white gave an increased feeling of height while the white gloss on the doors and banisters reflected additional light into what would otherwise have been a rather gloomy passageway.

DIAGNOSIS

This was rather a dark hall and the dark wood banisters did nothing to lead the eye upstairs. The clutter on the stairs added to the gloom, while the view straight into the kitchen was rather unappealing. A dark wooden table at the foot of the stairs added to the generally heavy, dated and drab feeling.

CURE

We painted the wooden banisters with white gloss, which brightened the space and led the eye up the stairs. If you really can't climb those stairs to put away the clutter, then invest in a few stylish baskets, which will at least hide the worst of the mess. The old table was replaced with a modern chrome trestle table in a style that bridged the gap between traditional and modern. Its surface also reflected the light – another plus in this hallway. Rather than displaying the kitchen in all its glory, we put up a fine curtain to screen it.

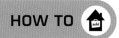 DISGUISE A BAD VIEW

If you want to retain your privacy or hide a bad view but let light in, avoid net curtains. Use fine fabrics such as muslins, voiles or unlined cotton. They fall well, let light filter through and are attractive. Consider using fabric that will cast a different light into the room and tone with its colour scheme. Antique lace pinned across a window gives a unique effect, but remember that direct sunlight will eventually damage it.

Left: Roll-up blinds provide privacy while still allowing light through.

blinds and shutters

Blinds are another good investment. Slatted Venetian blinds come in wood, metal or plastic in different colours and widths. Pulled down, the slats can be angled to control the amount of light flowing into a room. Their only disadvantage is that they can be awkward to clean. Plain roller blinds and Roman blinds can be made with fabrics that filter light and screen an unattractive view. Split-cane and bamboo blinds will add a rather colonial feel and look wonderful with the sun streaming through them.

Vertical louvre blinds are attached to the top and bottom of the window. Usually made of strips of canvas or wood, they pivot open and shut and pull open to the side. Café blinds or curtains cover only the lower half of a window, letting in light above it. Similarly, a type of roller blind can be fitted that rolls up from the bottom of the window. These can be pulled up to the right height to hide the view. Added interest can be given in a bay window by raising adjacent blinds to different heights. Louvred shutters are an alternative. They can be divided so that privacy is retained by only shutting the lower half.

using glass

Glass shelving can be fixed across a window and used to hold plants or ornaments, although this makes opening the window difficult, so ensure that it is not a window that you use often. These shelves will successfully obstruct the view, but light will still find its way in around them.

Frosted glass is often used in windows where privacy is particularly desired. If you want the effect without the cost, use a frosting spray. Having cleaned the windows thoroughly, the spray can be used to cover an entire pane or you might stencil a clear line around the edge of the window or patterns in the centre. Frosted film is another possibility. Stuck onto the window, it provides the same effect as frosted glass. For additional interest, or to admit more light, shapes or patterns can be cut out of it.

Churches are not the only preserve of stained or coloured glass. There are modern designs that lend themselves to domestic use. Subtle marbled patterns make a feature of a window while hiding what is behind. Coloured acetate makes a cheap and cheerful alternative. Again, a drawing on tracing paper can be an effective answer. If your room looks onto a brick wall allowing little or no light to come in, paint the wall a bright colour or paint a design or a mural on it to give something interesting to look at.

nifty trick

If little light comes into a basement room, attach an outdoor spotlight to the outside wall and angle it to shine in through the window. If you have covered the window to hide the view, it should look as if the sun has found a way to you after all and will provide more light than there was before.

Above: Frosted film can be stuck onto windows to achieve a frosted-glass effect. Shapes or patterns cut out of it provide additional interest.

LIVING & DINING ROOMS

It's important with living and dining rooms to make it clearly evident what they are each used for. Clear away clutter and have a good look at what's in both rooms. The living room is somewhere to relax in – make it a peaceful haven. Rearranging the furniture can often give the room a new lease of life, while putting away knickknacks, photos and ornaments will give the impression of space.

Dining rooms often double up as spare rooms, offices or playrooms, but if you want to sell your house you must display the room equipped for its primary function. A table laid with attractive crockery, cutlery and glasses will have immediate appeal. And don't forget finishing touches – fresh flowers and candles all suggest a lifestyle to aspire to.

LIVING ROOMS

Formal drawing rooms are a thing of the past, but that doesn't give you licence to present your living room as a pigsty, particularly when selling your house. Get rid of the junk, weed out crowded bookshelves and remove all evidence of your pets and any lingering smells.

Create a focal point. This is important in every room of the house, but especially in the living room, which is the one we want to feel most proud about.

There should be easy passage through the room, so check that the door isn't obstructed and that French windows are easily accessible.

Finally, a few well-chosen accessories in your accent colours will transform the space into a comfortable and desirable room.

TOP 10 TIPS

1 Hide all your family photos, golfing trophies or framed certificates. They only distract the viewers' attention away from the room and prevent them from making the crucial leap of seeing themselves living there.

2 Pay attention to the windows. Clean them, take away clutter that's obstructing the view and frame them with well-hung curtains or blinds.

3 Make a focal point of the fireplace, a special furniture grouping or even an interesting piece of art.

4 Tidy up the bookshelves. Group books in size order for a feeling of uniformity. To create a sense of space, leave room for one or two ornaments.

5 Arrange the furniture so there's easy passage through the room.

6 Having all the furniture lined up around the walls only makes the room look smaller and unwelcoming.

7 Good lighting can enhance the space and show off the room at its best.

8 Remove all evidence of pets and children. If that means removing the carpet too, then do it.

9 Don't forget to add finishing touches. Colour and life can be brought into the room by judicious use of cushions, rugs, pictures and flowers. Be careful not to overdo it, though.

10 Hide ugly radiators by boxing them in. This also provides a useful shelf for displaying one or two of your favourite ornaments.

The living room can show signs of too much life. If your buyer is going to be able to mentally move his own things in, you've got to make it easy for him by removing too much evidence of yourself and emphasising the room's potential. There should be easy passage through the room, so check the door isn't obstructed and that French windows are easily accessible. Too many pictures on the walls can be distracting for a buyer. We want them to be focusing on the finer points of the property you are attempting to sell, not undertaking a critique of your taste in art. Don't crowd the room with furniture or line it up around the walls – both make the room appear small and unwelcoming. Use the space to its best advantage. On the other hand, an empty room looks uncared-for and uninspiring, so look around the house for pieces of furniture to move into the room.

If the carpet's worn or has absorbed the smell of your pets, replace it. Again, a neutral colour is ideal. You can always brighten things up with a rug or two, which can go with you when you move.

House doctoring does not have to mean complete upheaval. A few minor adjustments can be more than enough to inject an indifferent room with a real touch of class in a short space of time.

REVAMP YOUR LIVING ROOM FOR...

Carpets, curtains, flooring and furniture are likely to be the main items of expenditure when updating your living room. Making fresh covers for sofas is cheaper than replacing the suite, while lurking under the old carpet might be a wooden floor just needing to be varnished. Boxing in radiators and updating the lighting will also immediately enhance the room.

UNDER £50	UNDER £100	UNDER £200
Paint walls and woodwork £20	Paint walls and woodwork £20	Paint walls and woodwork £20
Add a new rug £20	Add a new rug £20	Add a new rug £20
	Box in radiators £25	Box in radiators £25
	Hang a mirror and/or some pictures £30	Hang a mirror and/or some pictures £30
		Improve lighting £50
		Hang new curtains £45

Declutter

Dejunk thoroughly. Too much clutter will distract a buyer from seeing the properties of the room. Favourite ornaments and family photographs must all be thinned out to a bare minimum. You may love music, but must your CD collection cover the floor when there's all sorts of reasonably priced racking available? The same goes for books and videos. Then unearth a few choice ornaments from your cupboards and showcase them on the newly cleared shelves. TVs can dominate a room so if you can move the TV to a more discreet spot, then do so.

DIAGNOSIS

The amount of possessions crowded into this room was horrifying. There wasn't an inch of space left. So much stuff detracted from the two crucial selling points: the original beams and the size of the room itself. Too much furniture only added to that effect. Introducing some peace would restore some of the room's lost rustic charm.

CURE

Once we had got rid of the extraordinary amount of clutter the room immediately seemed to expand and became much lighter. The enormous fan gave the impression that the room might become unpleasantly hot in summer. Why put the idea into viewers' heads, particularly when they might enjoy a higher tolerance of heat? In place of the fan, I chose a large palm to add vitality and movement to the room. Then I plumped up the sofa cushions and covered the coffee table with a cloth and a vase of flowers, which gave focus to the area.

Decoration

If you've made a bold statement through your choice of wallpaper or paint, it makes sense to redecorate in a warm but neutral colour. Similarly, dated colour schemes do nothing for a room. When choosing to redecorate, colour coordinate carefully, using one colour as a base. An undercoat will be necessary if you are painting over dark colours.

DIAGNOSIS

This was a wonderfully proportioned room, but the dull carpet and multi-coloured walls and furnishings were hardly conducive to relaxing. The curtain pole cut across the Victorian gothic window and the single curtain gave a sense of imbalance. The fireplace was blocked by the television and attention was distracted by the untidy bookcase.

CURE

The walls were repainted in a strong but neutral colour and the sofas re-covered in a cream brocade; brightly coloured cushions added some colour to the room. Net hand-painted with fleurs-de-lys replaced the curtain, allowing the shape of the window to be seen. Under the carpet was a concrete floor, which, with special paint effects, was made to resemble an old flagged floor. We topped this with a large sisal mat. To emphasize the fireplace, the bookcase was cleared to the barest essentials, candles put in the grate and a new mirror hung.

DIAGNOSIS

The owner had painted the room herself, but in a gaudy orange that detracted from the more sophisticated atmosphere that a room like this should possess. The fireplace was hidden beneath an array of knickknacks, while the TV and videos dominated one corner of the room, which presented a problem because there was no obvious place to hide them.

CURE

First, we had to get rid of that ugly orange and repaint with a gentler, subtler shade. Then the room needed a really good clear out. Original features in a period house are almost always deemed selling points so it's wise to show them off. I made a screen to hide the television, cleared the mantelpiece and created a focal point by adding candles and some fresh flowers, with a mirror hung above. I had enough fabric left over from the screen to cover a small footstool. Peaceful and spacious, the room was now seen at its best.

Shelving

Weed out crowded bookshelves — overcrowding gives the impression that there isn't enough storage space in the room. Ornaments or vases can be used to break up shelf space, making it look bigger. If you have an empty alcove, put up some inexpensive laminated shelving to provide you with both storage and display space.

DIAGNOSIS

The messages given by this room were muddled. The Victorian fireplace sat uneasily beside the modern shelves and furniture. And although it's said that books furnish a room, they're not the only things that look good on shelves and there were just far too many of them. Weeding them out would give more emphasis to the fireplace.

CURE

The junk was moved from the shelves and mantelpiece, allowing the room to breathe. A new colour scheme dramatically altered the whole feel, making it more up-to-date and appealing. To underline the contemporary style of the room, accessories for the shelves were chosen especially to tone in with the colour scheme. But the Victorian fire surround didn't fit in with the new look. So specialist paints were used to hide the tiles and transform the whole thing into a modern fireplace that blended with the overall look of the room.

DISPLAY ITEMS

Displaying collections such as china, silver, tins or ornaments needs to be thought through carefully. Having too many pieces crammed into a space does neither the space nor the objects justice. All it shows is the impressive size of the collection and the fact that you don't have room to accommodate it. If necessary, rotate the collection so that it can be truly appreciated. A large collection can be displayed in different rooms.

pictures

If hung well, pictures lend character and warmth to a room. Single pictures may be hung symmetrically, possibly balancing a mirror or a piece of furniture. If you don't want a regimented sense of order then create a more asymmetrical look by visually balancing a large picture against a number of smaller ones, remembering that each side of the composition should take up the same square footage. When using pictures to create an impact, bear in mind that a strong unifying look can be achieved by using the same frames and mounts. If they are unevenly sized, the composition needs to be

worked out before hanging the pictures on the wall. Measure the wall space you want them to occupy then lay the pictures on the floor to occupy the right shape, working out the right balance. If unsure, make paper silhouettes and tape them to the wall first to see the effect.

books

Books furnish a room, but not if stuffed randomly into shelves or left on tables or the floor. They can give colour, texture and definition to a room if given proper space, so, when planning to house your books, think of shelving as a design feature not just a necessity. The inside of a bookcase might be painted a different colour to that of the walls, or wood stained to match the furniture. Objects displayed beside books will offset their shape and create a sense of depth and space.

Bookshelves can bring elements in a room together. They can frame doors or windows, unifying the spaces between them. They can also act as a focal point – for example, cubed shelves arranged in a geometric pattern against a wall. They can also frame a focal point if, for example, they are built into alcoves on either side of a chimney breast. If buying furniture, think about how it might be used for books – a small bookcase can double as an occasional table by a sofa. Or a sofa might back onto a low bookcase rather than a table. The space beneath a window seat or bed could be converted into bookshelves. A wide passage between rooms or a stairway might be transformed by floor-to-ceiling bookcases. Remember, this sort of library needs to be well lit so that it doesn't seem poky and so that its contents can be seen. Wherever the shelves, do not overcrowd them – weed out books you're unlikely to read again and give them to charity.

Windows

If the room has a good outlook, frame the windows with curtains and make sure nothing in the room blocks out the view. If you've got French windows, make sure they are easy to get to. If the view isn't so good, avoid net curtains. They are rather old-fashioned and look terrible as soon as they get even slightly dirty. Instead find a way to dress the window that will hide what's outside while still letting in light — bamboo blinds are good, or use muslin or voile.

DIAGNOSIS

This room simply didn't look like a home. The uncurtained windows and bare light bulbs did nothing for the feel. Nor did the amount of clutter accumulated on the small tables. Meanwhile, one end was just dead space with nothing going on in it whatsoever, and, above, yellow cornicing drew the eye upwards, towards the offending lights.

CURE

To emphasise the sensational view we decided on a strong but simple window treatment. A pair of curtains to tone with the gold in the rest of the room framed the view perfectly, making the room more homely. The iron pole was deliberately longer than the window so that, when pulled back, the curtains didn't block either the view or the light. A streamlined uplighter, to the left of the window, attracted the eye to that end of the room while, on the other side, the television was tucked into the corner, the flowers distracting from its presence.

DIAGNOSIS

This room was set in a stunning period property, but I felt the living room lacked a sense of comfort. The furnishings at the window area and the blood-red walls were too strong and personal, and the roller blinds hardly did justice to such a wonderful bay. The way that the furniture was arranged made the space seem smaller than it was, too.

CURE

The window was an important feature in the room, but I felt it was underexploited. Bright red could have been offputting to buyers, so I toned the area down with a light green that blended in with the rest of the room. The windows themselves were imposing enough to deserve special treatment, so we ordered custom-made blinds, which transformed the bay into a more elegant and inviting spot. By moving the existing furniture around, removing some and thinning out the contents of the shelves, the room immediately felt larger.

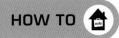
DRESS WINDOWS

Curtains have many uses – they frame and enhance a window and its view, they help keep the warmth in a room, they act as a shield between you and the world outside and they control the amount of light that enters. Blinds give a clean, uncluttered look on their own, but can also work well with curtains to provide privacy or shade. They are particularly useful where curtains are hard to fit, for instance in dormer windows.

Above: By extending the curtain pole beyond the width of the window, curtains can be drawn clear, allowing maximum light in.

curtains

The style of curtain you choose should relate to the style of your room. Take into account the period of your house, the style of your furniture and the existing décor of the room. Take your time in choosing the fabric. Make sure to take sample swatches home so you can test them in the light of the room and against your colour scheme. The ideal curtain length is either to the floor or to the windowsill. Anything in between will not flatter the proportions of the window. Never skimp on fabric to save money. Generous curtains look best, so choose cheaper fabric rather than less of it. Large patterns suit big windows and heavy fabrics work best full-length. If you're stuck, try plain cream curtains edged with coordinating fabric. You can play with the dimensions of the window by your choice of curtain. A narrow window will look wider if the curtain rail is extended on either side and sill-length curtains are used, while a wide window can be narrowed with floor-length curtains and/or those that cover part of the glass when open.

curtain accessories

So often in interior design it is the details that count. Curtains must fit, but headings, pelmets and poles should be combined to maximum effect.

HEADINGS

Headings are the different kinds of gathers at the top of the curtain, and are often determined by the kind of heading tape used. The most simple is a gathered heading about 2.5cm (1in) deep. Pencil pleats (about 7.5cm/3in deep running continuously across the curtain) and pinch pleats (small groups of pleats occurring at regular intervals) are the most popular. For a more formal effect, you might use box pleats, goblet pleats or lattice pleats. Other types of headings include looped, or tab-top, headings (loops, or tabs, that circle the pole), cased headings (in which two parallel rows of stitching across the top hem create a slot for a curtain pole), wooden, plastic or metal rings sewn directly onto the fabric or simple fabric ties.

TRACKS AND POLES

Take as much time to choose your curtain poles or tracks as the curtains themselves. Poles can be plain or decorative and come in a huge range of materials and diameters. Make sure the track or pole is strong enough to bear the weight of your chosen fabric.

PELMETS

Pelmets cover the curtain headings or tracks and can be as simple or as fancy as the mood takes. They are usually made of wood and can be cut into shapes that complement the window. Covered with fabric or just painted, they define the window and can help make a formal statement.

TIEBACKS

These are particularly useful to hold the curtains back out of the way. Whether you want a simple metallic or wooden holdback or a more elaborate fabric tie will depend on the style of your curtains. Tiebacks can be richly tasselled ropes or made of the same fabric as the curtain or pelmet, or made of contrasting fabric.

Lighting

The way you light a room can make the world of difference to it and can instantly add style and atmosphere. Dimmer switches are ideal for creating different moods, while mobile Anglepoise lamps can be used as uplighters to create an ambient glow, or you can use them as a task light to shed light over an armchair for easy reading. Table lamps can illuminate dark corners and alcoves or highlight a special vase or plant, while wall lights can throw light up or down, or onto a painting hung below them. Coordinate lampshades to match the main theme or as an accent colour. If you have chandeliers, do give them a thorough clean until they sparkle. Candles add to the ambience, but make sure they are new and not half-used. If rooms are open plan match the light fittings in each to visually link them.

HOW TO 🏠 CREATE A FOCAL POINT

Every room needs a focal point. It is the element that grounds the space and focuses your attention on entering. It gives the room a centre, and brings disparate elements together. Display it well, arranging furniture and artefacts around it. It is possible to have more than one focal point in a room as long as one is subordinate. A fireplace may be highlighted in the winter, while a plant or picture window may be the summer's focus.

fireplaces

If your room does have a beautiful fireplace, make the most of it. Remove any clutter that may be obscuring it, clean it thoroughly and polish any fire irons or surround. Clear the mantelpiece of accumulated photographs and invitations and arrange only one or two objects in their place. Hang a large mirror or picture above so that the eye is not distracted by too many different elements. A fire always gives the subliminal message that the living room is the heart of the home, but burning candles in the grate can be equally attractive. Arrange the furniture around it, so that it becomes the unmistakable centrepiece of the room.

feature windows

Another focal point might be a stunning view through a window. Emphasise it by dressing the window appropriately. It might be enough just to paint the window frame a contrasting colour. Otherwise there are all sorts of blinds, curtains and drapes that could be used (see How to Dress Windows, page 70). When dressing the window take into account its size and the style of the rest of the room. Swags and tails will not look good in a minimalist environment or on a modest casement window. Other ways of drawing attention to the window might include the addition of a built-in bay window seat, window boxes on the outside ledge, a single table in front of it or an ornament on the ledge. Again, it is important to orientate the furniture so that the view isn't blocked by anything too large and can be seen from all vantage points in the room.

ALTERNATIVE FOCAL POINTS

If your room is not blessed with either a fireplace or a view, consider using the largest piece of furniture as a focal point. Ensure that the piece is positioned correctly: if the room is symmetrical the focal point should be placed centrally. Tables should be beautifully laid or have a central decoration or runner. Beds should be made with clean linen with scatter cushions accentuating the colour scheme; cupboard doors should be shut with nothing hanging from them and dressers should display only a select number of objects. Sometimes a striking artwork can be used as a focal point. This can take the form of a single picture or of a carefully arranged group (see How to Display Items, page 67).

Fireplaces and radiators

If your living room has a fireplace, make sure this area makes a statement that complements the style of the house. Fireplaces should be swept and mantelpieces cleared of all but a couple of items. A blazing fire always looks welcoming, but remember to empty the grate when it's out. If the fireplace is modern, considering adding a surround and mantel, if it's in keeping with the rest of the house. Hang a mirror or picture above the fireplace to emphasise its importance as a feature in the room. If the fireplace is filled with an old-fashioned heater, investigate replacing it with something more up-to-date.

DIAGNOSIS

This fireplace should have been at the heart of the room, but the owner had clearly lost all interest here. The room had no warmth and gave no subliminal invitation to sit down and relax. There was nowhere near enough furniture and the walls needed a good clean. It was essential to make this room look as if it were lived in.

CURE

Just adding a mirror immediately broke up the expanse of wall and helped to make the fireplace the focal point of the room, as it should have been. Without furniture, the room was in real trouble until we borrowed the cupboard and occasional table. The natural tones of wood contrast effectively with the brick fireplace and balance the room superbly. Ambience was what this room lacked, so we injected colour with a rug and cushions, then added plants, potpourri, scented candles and selected ornaments and the room was alive again.

DIAGNOSIS

Sometimes fireplaces can be too overwhelming. The massive, brick fireplace completely dominated the room, making it seem narrower and darker. The deep red carpet and curtains only contributed to the same feeling. Clutter had accumulated on every surface, including the fire grate. I had my work cut out to restore the rural charm this room had lost.

CURE

To reduce the effect of the heavy red brick on the chimney I painted it with a mix of watered-down white emulsion before sanding it back to give a rustic, weathered appearance. This made the fireplace apparently recede and the room seem bigger. Hanging a circular mirror on the chimney breast broke up its dominant, angular lines and helped to create the illusion of space and light. We replaced the dark carpet, changed the curtains for simple cream ones and cleared the clutter. Toning cushions provided the final lift to the room.

FIREPLACES AND RADIATORS

A fireplace can definitely add value to your home. It always provides an interesting focal point to a room, as well as being a practical heating source. Any existing fireplace should be properly cleaned and you should make sure that it's not being blocked from view by any furniture. If the surround doesn't fit the period of the house, visit an architectural salvage yard where you may be able to pick up something suitable at a reasonable price. If the fireplace has been boxed in, it's often worthwhile restoring it to its former glory. The same goes for that empty hole left when one has been removed. You could complete the look by investing in a fireguard and fire dogs. Light the fire if it's appropriate. Remove all the invitations and general junk from the mantelpiece where there is room for a well-chosen ornament or two – at most! Complete the look by hanging a large mirror or painting above.

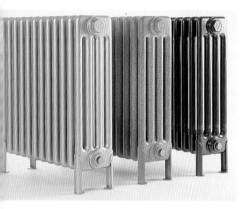

Above: Traditional styles of radiator can be used as a feature in themselves – there's no need to box them in.

Make sure that the radiators are working and the house is warm in the winter. Don't block them with furniture or curtains. Contemporary radiators and reclaimed industrial radiators can make a strong design statement, but unless you've deliberately bought your radiators with that in mind you will probably have standard functional wall fittings that add nothing to a room. However, you can change that. Boxing them in is a very simple job. If the paintwork is chipped or you want to make more or less of a feature of them, there is a wide range of specialist radiator paints available.

- Use the finest grade wet and dry paper to take surface discolouration off a marble surround. Wet the paper and use very carefully.

- A decent brand of instant coffee mixed with a little water will stain a wood surround or match paler patches.

- Rake out the grouting between tiles and regrout before washing the tiles with soapy water.

- Black grout is a good idea for fireplace tiles – smoke won't stain it. Alternatively, stain the existing grout black.

- Repolish all cast-iron work with graphite paste.

- Put up a shelf over your radiator to stop the walls above getting dirty.

Top left: Instead of the trouble and expense of restoring an old fireplace, a feature can still be made using a fire surround.

Top right: A blazing fire never fails to give heart to a home.

Bottom left: A fireplace is the perfect centrepiece to a room, with a mantelpiece to display favourite ornaments.

Bottom right: Radiator paints can be used to give a new lease of life to an old radiator. Alternatively, there are modern, coloured replacements.

SELL IT!

Elbow grease can add more value to your house than almost anything else. I can't over-emphasise how important it is to clean, clean and clean some more when you're selling your house. The kitchen and the bathroom are the two most important rooms to get absolutely spotless, but it shouldn't stop there. Dust every surface, ornament and lampshade that you possess. Make sure that the ashes are removed from the fireplace and that a fire is newly laid. The fire surround, whether tiles, slate or marble, should be positively gleaming.

Flooring

If the carpet is in an overwhelming design or in terrible condition, consider replacing it with a neutral plain one. Or look underneath — the existing floorboards may be in a good enough condition to sand and varnish — a cheap, but effective solution. Wood has a natural warmth that suits almost any room. Wooden floors also give a lighter, more up-to-the-minute look, and can easily be warmed up with the addition of a colourful rug or two.

DIAGNOSIS

This room was a mess. The brown carpet was horribly drab and dull, while grubby old net curtains were teamed with ugly floral curtains that didn't fit the window. A mismatched table and the usual clutter just added to the overall impression of a tip.

CURE

Unfortunately, the floorboards under the carpet weren't quite good enough to sand and varnish. However, a useful alternative is to paint them with specialist paint. Check that there aren't any nails sticking out and that the surface is smooth, clean and dry before you apply it. Painted white, they immediately brightened the room. The nets were replaced by Venetian blinds and teamed with muslin curtains to frame the window. A new coffee table looked more contemporary than the last and doubled as a cunning CD storage unit.

When I first walked into this room, my head span. It was a riot of patterns, pinks and reds. It was overwhelming. Apart from the bright colours, jangling patterns leapt from the carpets, wallpaper border, furniture fabric, wall stencils, lace curtains, teapot collection and general clutter. Everything needed to be toned down if a buyer was to feel calm and at home. Only then would he or she be able to focus on the house itself and how it might be adapted to suit other furniture and colour schemes. The swirling patterned red carpet was shown the skip and in came a chic new beige-coloured substitute. The walls were painted a soft clean colour to obliterate the pinks, the border and stencils. I did allow another border back into the room, but it was much more discreet than the last and served to break up the bare expanses of wall.

BEFORE

AFTER

Furniture

If your rooms look rather empty, buy, borrow or rent furniture until you move – new furniture will look better and can go with you to your new home. Move furniture around until the area looks spacious and uncrowded. Pieces from other rooms may help. If a sofa dominates the room, leaving little space for anything else, it may be worth replacing it with a smaller model to give a greater feeling of spaciousness. Tired old sofas and armchairs that look as if they've lost their bounce can be brought back to life fairly simply and inexpensively with smart throws, slipcovers, or the addition of coloured cushions. Cushions come in limitless sizes and shapes and are useful for introducing colour, texture and a feeling of comfort. They can coordinate or contrast with the other surfaces and colours in a room and can be used to inject a bit of zip into a depressed piece of furniture.

If a more drastic cover-up is needed, the easiest thing is to cover either a sofa or an armchair with a throw. There is a large range of designs and colours available to transform not only the furniture but the whole look of a room. If you don't want to go to the expense of buying a throw, good alternatives are bedspreads, rugs, antique and modern shawls. All of these have the advantage of protecting the sofa from further damage, disguising the damage that has already been done and introducing colour and texture into a room. A disadvantage is that they will slip out of place unless firmly secured.

A throw can be simply draped over the piece of furniture and held in place by cushions. Greater security is achieved by tucking it into the sides and back of the sofa. To make sure your throw is big enough to do this, measure the sofa from front to back adding at least another 30cm (12in) to accommodate the tuck, and from side to side adding another 60cm (24in). Don't skimp. Alternatively, use one throw for the back of the sofa, another for the seat and others over the arms. Small, specialist spiral pins are sold to hold throws in place.

A more expensive solution is to make or buy loose covers. They will give your sofa or chair a new look at less cost than buying a new one. Stick to medium-weight fabrics and, if the covers are washable, check they are shrinkproof. To look their best they need to be carefully measured and fitted, although if you are lucky you may find the perfect off-the-peg solution.

Dining-room chairs can also be given a new lease of life. If they are wooden, they can be touched up with woodstain and varnish, or painted. Add colour and comfort by adding cushions, perhaps even with ties to fasten to the chairback and legs. If the seat is removable, a new cover is the answer. It is a simple matter to remove the seat, lay it upside down on a new piece of fabric, then pull the fabric taut over the top and tack or staple it in place underneath, carefully pleating the corners before neatening the base by covering it with a piece of plain tough fabric.

Another solution is a simple slip-over cover that reaches to just below the seat or to the floor. Made from a pattern of squares and rectangles, a simple slipcover may have inverted pleats over each leg, button-up backs or tied sides or back.

When choosing new fabric, remember what else is in the room when you look at different textures, colours and patterns. If you are unsure in your choice, it is often wise to go for a neutral colour, relying on its texture for interest. Then, when it is in situ, dress it up with a coloured cushion or two that will tie it in with the general colour scheme.

DIAGNOSIS

More a padded cell than a living room, this room couldn't have been presented less invitingly. The furniture had seen many years of use and had been packed around the walls as a safety net for a toddler. This only had the effect of making the space appear smaller. Children's toys, general junk, and family photos littered the surfaces.

CURE

I decided to replace the furniture. I usually try to use other pieces in the house, but in this case I was unlucky. The piano came in from the dining room, but the owners had to invest in a new sofa, table and rug, all of which would suit their new home, too. The carpet had seen better days, but underneath it the existing floorboards were in a good enough condition to sand and varnish. The walls were repainted a light, fresh shade of green and we colour coordinated the accessories so the dark green accents tied together the different surfaces.

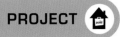
NEW-LOOK SOFA

Don't show a favourite old sofa the dump. A new loose cover will bring it back to life, making it a welcome part of any decorative scheme.

What you need

- sofa in need of covering
- old sheet or cotton fabric for pattern
- large pins
- fabric marker pen
- scissors
- tape measure
- fabric for finished cover
- matching thread
- fastenings

make pattern

To make a loose-fitting sofa cover, you will need to make a pattern first from an old sheet or piece of fabric.

ONE Outside arms: Pin the fabric against the outside arm, smoothing it and repinning it so that it is a close fit. With a fabric marker pen, draw the line of the seam. Repeat with the other arm.

TWO Outside back: Cut two pattern pieces allowing a 10cm (4in) overlap down the centre. Pin them onto the back of the sofa, folding back the

3

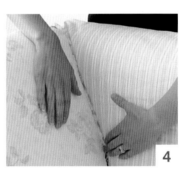

4

facings for the centre opening. Smooth the fabric out to the side and pin. Draw the seam lines and the centre fold on the fabric, ensuring the two pieces overlap properly. Remove and machine tack the two back seams. Replace the fabric on the sofa.

THREE Inside arms: Cut a piece allowing enough fabric to tuck into the side of the sofa and for shaping around the corners. Pin to the sofa along the seam line on the outer arm (left). Smooth the fabric over the arm

and into the tuck. Mark the seam lines along the arm and down the front edge of the sofa. Push the pen between the seat and the arm to mark the seam line of the tuck-in.

FOUR Inside back: Cut a section of fabric and pin it to the outside back along the top seam line. Smooth the fabric across the back so that it tucks down into the seat and arms (left). Push the pen into the sides and seat to mark the tuck-in.

FIVE To get the fabric fitting neatly, make a dart at the top corners of the

5

sofa. Smooth the material towards the corner and cut off the extra (opposite below). Pin the seams, making sure they fit snugly.

SIX Unpin the material from the sofa and sew the seams, easing the corner seams by cutting them where necessary. Replace the cover on the sofa to check the fit. Trim off any surplus material and make any adjustments to the seams by remarking and resewing. Cross out the old lines to avoid any muddle (below).

6

SEVEN Seat and front skirt: Should be cut as one piece, allowing extra to tuck in at the back and sides of the sofa. Smooth the fabric from the back forwards, pinning in place and marking the seam lines, pushing the pen into the tucks. Pin the sides of the skirt to the arms of the sofa to check the size. Remove and machine tack to the back and arms. Put back on the sofa.

EIGHT Front arms: Cut the fabric and place on the sofa. Smooth and pin

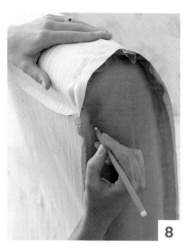

8

from the top downwards. Use a dart if necessary. Mark the seams (above). Repeat for the other arm.

NINE Remove the cover from the sofa and machine tack the last seams. Trim the seam allowances to 2cm ($^3/_4$in). Turn the cover the right side out and replace it on the sofa, working from the front backwards (below). If it doesn't fit anywhere, remark the seams, crossing out the previous lines. Remove and restitch if necessary.

9

cut out pattern

TEN Check every seam line is marked. Check every section is marked with its name and that it is clear which is the right side of the fabric. Unpick the cover by cutting along the seam lines. Place the pattern pieces on the furnishing fabric and carefully mark the seam lines, remembering to check the position of any pattern. Cut out the fabric making sure you leave a seam allowance all the way round.

make cover

ELEVEN Follow steps 1–9 again, using the furnishing fabric. Sew the hem by hand and finish the opening at the centre back with velcro, buttons, a zip, loops or ties.

SEAT CUSHIONS

For each seat cushion cut out two pieces of fabric the size of the cushion top plus seam allowances. Cut one long strip the size of three sides plus seam allowances. Cut two pieces the length of one side and half the depth plus seam allowances and sew a zipper between them. Sew the short ends of the strips together, right sides facing. Sew the band to the cushion top, right sides facing. Next, with the zip half open, sew the band to the cushion bottom. Trim the seams, turn the cover the right side out through the zip and insert the cushion.

DINING ROOMS

If you have a separate room that functions purely as a dining room, then ensure it looks as friendly and inviting as the rest of the house. The dining room is often one of the most under-utilised rooms in the home, or it may double as anything from a home office to a children's playroom or even a temporary bedroom. But that's not what potential buyers want to see.

By smartening up your dining room and defining its function, you will give people an opportunity to imagine what life might be like if they buy your house. Remember, staging your home is all about promoting and selling a lifestyle, and dining rooms can often seem rather characterless since they're comparatively rarely used.

TOP 10 TIPS

1 If you are fortunate enough to have a separate dining room, don't let it double as an office, playroom or box room while your home is being marketed.

2 Avoid clutter, especially on the table and tops of furniture, so that people will find it easy to imagine themselves sitting down to enjoy a meal there.

3 If you need to freshen up the walls choose colours that are warm and invite dining and entertaining. If using wallpaper, be sure that it is not too busy or overpowering.

4 Don't crowd the room with furniture. It should be easy to walk round the table.

5 Freshen up old dining chairs with smart new seat covers or add small, comfortable cushions.

6 Cover a particularly tatty table with a new tablecloth or table runner.

7 If there is no separate dining room, find a space that could be used as a dining area and define it with table and chairs.

8 If you haven't got a table and chairs, beg, borrow or hire them – this is an essential part of selling a lifestyle.

9 Fresh flowers in a beautiful vase in the centre of the table will give it focus.

10 Lay the table with coordinating napkins and china, issuing a subliminal invitation to your viewer, but keep it simple, please.

The colour scheme should be warm and inviting, not busy or overpowering, so consider repainting or laying a new carpet. If the room doubles as an office, playroom or whatever, then relocate any items that don't fit a dining room's function. Or, at the very least, try to screen them off.

As with every other room, it's essential to clear out any clutter and to clean the room thoroughly. Smarten up the table and chairs — polish table tops and clean chair seats. If necessary, recover the seats and if your table has seen better days cover it with an attractive cloth or runner. Set the table with good crockery, cutlery and glasses — this will reinforce the purpose of the room in the buyer's eye. Don't forget light switches and door handles — simply changing them to reflect the period of the house can really improve the room. It's always worth paying attention to such details. If the walls look empty, hang a mirror (good feng shui) or some pictures, and if you have chairs crammed round the table, remove a couple to give the impression of space and comfort. Most of all, clear away the remains of the last meal, including the ketchup bottle, salt and pepper. Nothing looks worse.

REVAMP YOUR DINING ROOM FOR...

Allow for repainting the walls and ceiling. Get the carpet professionally cleaned, or consider replacing it. Invest in some new dining room furniture, if necessary, and coordinate finishing touches. Replacement light switches, lampshades and door handles can all give a fresher feel.

UNDER £50		UNDER £100		UNDER £200	
Replace seat covers	£20	Paint walls and woodwork	£40	Paint walls and woodwork	£40
Clean carpet	£20	Replace seat covers	£20	Replace seat covers	£20
		Clean carpet	£20	Clean carpet	£20
		Buy new place mats	£10	Buy new place mats	£10
		Stain or paint old dining table and chairs	£10	Stain or paint old dining table and chairs	£10
				Hire a sander for the day and strip the floorboards	£50

Define the space

The function of each room in the home must be clearly spelled out. A dining room is particularly important because it implies that a certain kind of desirable lifestyle is on offer. A dining room is for eating in – not watching television, playing computer games or sewing curtains. It should be an uncluttered, welcoming room with matching furniture and calming decor.

DIAGNOSIS

Who would believe this was a dining room? It had a little bit of everything – wine cellar, office, playroom. Children's toys littered the floor and balloons from a long-forgotten party hung from light fittings. This is no way to present any room. We had to define the dining room so that it would add value to the house by giving it that extra space.

CURE

This messy, multi-functional room was completely cleared and the walls painted a neutral shade, while the carpet was replaced with a soothing plain one. The owners had no appropriate furniture so we bought a light wood table and chairs. Attention should be clearly focussed on the table, and by placing it in the centre of the room the window was no longer blocked. Having cleaned the window, we hung new curtains in a light, floral fabric, which visually linked the room to the outside. The room felt and looked much lighter.

Flooring

If you have carpet in the dining room, ensure that it is clean, or get it professionally cleaned. A brightly patterned carpet won't be to everyone's taste, so consider replacing it with something more neutral or, if the floorboards are sound, sand and varnish the surface, using a mixture of sawdust and specialist sealing compound to fill any gaps. If your carpet has seen better days, have a look underneath — sometimes a beautiful parquet floor lies below. This can be revitalised by vigorously cleaning with one part turpentine, one part vinegar and one part methylated spirits, then waxing.

DIAGNOSIS

That green carpet must be one of the brightest I've seen during my whole time as House Doctor. Although the owner was keen on golf, having your own putting green indoors is going too far. It dominated the room and could make any buyer turn tail. I also wasn't keen on the leggy plant that was climbing the trellis or the unattractive pot it was planted in.

CURE

The carpet had to go. Since the walls were a neutral colour, we compromised on a less strident green on the floor.
The plant did nothing except provide an obstacle to get round. Without it, we removed the trellis to reveal the frosted glass, which lent a sense of connection with the adjoining room. I moved the music stand closer to the piano and opened the sheet music, then the bare dining table was improved by the addition of a flowering plant that toned in with the chair seats and curtains and gave focus.

DIAGNOSIS

The carpet in this busy dining room was the owner's favourite, but the pattern was so strong that it ran the risk of repelling any viewer. The walls were hung with fussy wallpaper and decorative plates. The dining chairs were mismatched, while an ugly 1950s cabinet, a sideboard and cupboards all groaned under the weight of knickknacks. I had to lighten, brighten and declutter.

CURE

The carpet was replaced with seagrass matting, a cost-effective solution to flooring in any period of house. I removed the cabinet and armchair to give more space and moved the sideboard. The walls were stripped and a dado rail added. I chose hard-wearing anaglypta paper, with a muted heritage paint below and a paler shade above. A large picture replaced the plates on the wall and the contents of the cupboards were thinned out.

The table was polished and dressed and the unmatching chairs removed. The room was now uniform in character and looking twice its original size.

FLOORING

The choice and condition of your floor coverings say a lot about you to the buyer. Make sure it's all good by looking at the carpet and asking yourself if something else wouldn't look better. Take the period of your house into consideration. A hip rubber floor will look quite wrong in a Georgian town house, while wall-to-wall carpet may look out of place in the most modern house. There's a huge range of carpets and other materials to choose from, so before you replace, think about what the room is used for. Also

Above: A floating hardwood floor provides a clean and modern finish for all rooms.

remember that, ideally, you're not going to live with it forever, so don't go for the bright red or sunshine yellow that you love. Choose the plain, the neutral, the understated. These won't offend a buyer's eye and have the advantage of apparently enlarging the floor space too. Seagrass matting can be a practical alternative, if a little unfriendly to bare feet and crawling babies. Should the idea of buying carpet be too daunting, look at the floorboards beneath. Bare varnished boards often look great with a couple of rugs thrown on them. Rugs are a good way of bringing together the colour scheme in a room, too. In the kitchen or bathroom, the floors should clean up thoroughly or you should replace the covering. Whatever you use should be waterproof and hard-wearing. Again, there's a huge range of choice, but err on the side of the neutrals. The flooring should always recede into the background, letting your furnishings speak for themselves.

- Remember what the room is being used for when you choose the floor covering.
- Replace kitchen and bathroom carpet with something hard-wearing and easy to clean – perhaps tiles (vinyl or ceramic), lino or wood.
- You will need a hard-wearing carpet for the hall and stairway.
- A dark staircase and hall can often be dramatically improved by a lighter neutral shade of carpet.
- Choose neutral colours so the carpet fades into the background.
- Stain and varnish floorboards or paint them with specialist hard-wearing paint.

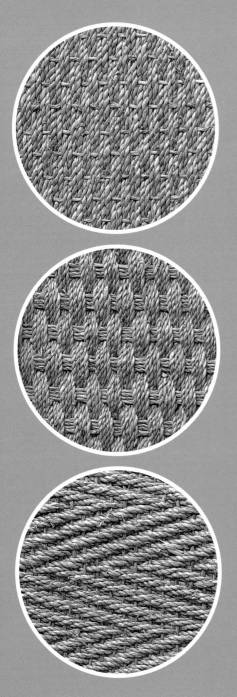

Left top, middle, bottom: Coir matting comes in different weaves that provide interest in an otherwise neutral floor covering. It is hard-wearing and ideal for any room except kitchen and bathroom.

Above: Linoleum has come a long way since the 1950s.

Above right: Amtico floor tiles offer an excellent, hard-wearing, easy-to-clean finish.

Right: A combination of Amtico and hardwood offers a floor treatment with a difference.

SELL IT!

Your carpet can play a big role in a successful house sale. A carpet that is dark or heavily patterned dominates a room and makes it seem smaller. A smelly, damp carpet is a real bathroom turn-off. Dining rooms with food trodden into the floor are out. The same goes if the carpet is old, worn or just dirty. A new carpet may seem an unnecessary expense, but it will lift the appearance of the room and your buyers won't be imagining the extra cost of replacing it themselves. Make it easy for them to like your house.

CARE FOR WOODEN FLOORS

Flooring has a tremendous impact on a room. Whether in a traditional or sleek contemporary setting, wooden flooring imparts a natural warmth and style of its own. By definition, it suffers a great deal of wear and tear from everyday use from shoes, furniture or spillages, so it is essential to look after it well if it is to retain its good looks.

treating minor damage

Before treating any minor damage, find out how the boards have been treated. The traditional finishes of oil and wax are the easiest to repair because they make it relatively straightforward to get to the wood. Superficial damage can usually be remedied by rubbing in paste wax with extra-fine wire wool. If the damage is a result of pressure from heavy furniture, try covering it with a damp cloth, then ironing it. The hot moisture should encourage the wood fibres to expand to their original shape. Keep stiletto heels at bay at all costs.

A polyurethane finish is harder to damage, but any damage is also harder to treat. First lightly sand the area without cutting into the wood itself. Gently wipe away any dust. Use a paint pad to apply the new polyurethane and thin out towards the edges with a dry brush. Water-based polyurethane gives a clear finish, while oil-based polyurethane will darken with age.

restoring an original floor

If you have discovered a wooden floor under an old carpet, more drastic action will probably be needed. Do not underestimate the amount of work it will take to achieve a really sound attractive finish. Call in the professionals if you have doubts about your own staying power. First sink any loose nails, secure loose boards or replace rotten ones. If the floor is in really good condition, you may be able to get away with sanding by hand, but more likely you will need to hire a sanding machine and an edge sander to take off accumulated dirt, worn paint or polish. This is a noisy and dirty job and will take some time. Vacuum up the resulting dust and clean the boards with white spirit.

TREATING FLOORS

Once stripped, there are a number of treatments to choose from – paint, varnish or woodstain. Whichever finish you choose, you can be sure that it will be a lasting, natural solution that will add value to your home.

● Sealing

Unless the floor is painted, it will need sealing properly for protection. Among the various sealants available there are oils, waxes and, most popular, polyurethane. A properly sealed floor should be easy to clean, needing only a good sweep or vacuum and a wipe with a damp mop. Try to avoid getting it too wet. Long-term maintenance may be a little more troublesome. An oiled or waxed finish will probably need to be renewed after a couple of months. A sealed floor has a much longer life, but if it begins to get a bit worn it may need refinishing to prevent the wood being damaged by dirt and moisture.

● Painting

Before painting, be sure to prime the floor well before using a hard-wearing gloss, floor or deck paint. Primer is not necessary if you are liming the floor. If liming, give the floor a good scrub with a dry brush to open up the grain, work the liming agent (white paint, liming wax or gesso) into the wood with steel wool, wipe away any surplus then seal with polyurethane. Staining is another option that does not require a primer, but remember to use several coats of varnish for a really hard, protective finish.

Furniture

Keep the furniture in the room to a minimum so that it's possible to walk around or sit at the table with ease. If your table has doubled as a desk or a work surface, cover it with a smart tablecloth or runner.

Look at your dining room chairs. If you can, make sure they match and that the seat covers are not showing the remains of previous parties. Making new seat covers for loose seats is an inexpensive and simple job. Simple cushions are another way to give an impression of comfort. The fabric should tie in with the colours of the curtains or even repeat it.

DIAGNOSIS

Who'd want to eat in here? The chairs that didn't match and crumpled tablecloth gave a cheerless impression. Everything about this room made you want to pass swiftly through it into the conservatory beyond – although the view of the washing basket was a turnoff. And the framed posters are too reminiscent of student days – they would have to go.

CURE

To entice people to sit at this table, we replaced the tablecloth with a rich but neutral-coloured runner, which showed it off at its best. Putting a decoration in its centre gave the whole thing focus. The old seat covers were drab so were re-covered quite cheaply, and gave the impression of a new suite. A framed print was hung on one wall and an iron screen with toning fabric panels was placed against the other wall; it broke up the space and lent softness to the room. The washing was removed, and candles completed the look.

DIAGNOSIS

This room was crowded with antiques. Having the table in the middle of the room meant that, although it could be easily got at, the fireplace was blocked from view, and the cluttered alcoves on either side also detracted from it. The combination of curtains and Viennese blinds was definitely too much of a good thing and made the room seem smaller.

CURE

The task here was obvious – to thin out the furniture and show off the size of the room and its principal features. Placing the dining table against the wall wasn't ideal since it would have to be moved every mealtime, but we compromised so that the fireplace could be seen in all its glory. With the jumble edited down on each side and a single picture on the mantel shelf, it became the rightful focal point. We freshened up the room with a couple of coats of paint and removed the curtains. Without them, the blind looked much better.

LIGHTS AND SWITCHES

Lighting can make an enormous difference to the appearance of a room. A bare light bulb swinging from the ceiling not only looks awful, it makes everything else in the room look

Above: A standard lamp and a table lamp provide useful background lighting.

awful, too. So, before you go any further, look at the lighting you have and see how it can be improved. Dusty, tired or faded lampshades should be replaced immediately. Alternatives do not have to be expensive or elaborate, but they will certainly improve the look of the room. It may be better to go for a warmer, creamy shade than a white one, which can create a much colder effect. Or you might consider swapping a standard daytime bulb with a warm-toned bulb (red or orange), which will give a completely different sort of light. Central ceiling lights in a living room or bedroom are never as complimentary or as atmospheric as a range of table lamps or a pair of bedside lamps, which will be much softer. Where possible, angle the light so that it falls on areas used for activities in the room and hides the bits you'd rather weren't seen.

In the kitchen it's important to ensure that your working areas are adequately lit. Clip-on spotlights or a track of halogen downlighters may be a worthwhile investment. Candlelight can be both flattering and dramatic. Throw out any half-burned stubs and arrange new candles to give some extra atmosphere. Nor is it expensive to replace your switches with dimmers, which give you the advantage of being able to alter the strength of lighting in the room to suit the time of day.

- Look at cleaning up existing light fittings before investing in new ones.
- If you are going to replace, first define your period.
- Decide whether you're going with authentic or repro materials.
- Use officially approved materials.
- Ensure that all wiring is sound.
- Shop around for your switches and light fittings. The first ones you find are not always the best or the cheapest.
- Use a properly qualified electrician.

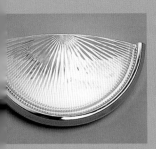

Top left: An uplighter is a good way of achieving ambient light.

Top middle: A single spot is useful for highlighting a particular area or object.

Top right: A downlighter is another way of providing ambient light.

Middle: A tracking system of halogen spotlights is ideal for lighting a kitchen.

Bottom left: Three spots can simultaneously light different areas of the same room.

Bottom right: Choose your switches to suit the period and style of your home. There is a huge range to choose from.

SELL IT!

A favourite trick of mine is to use a mirror wherever I can. Apart from adding space to a room, a carefully placed mirror also maximises the available light. Ensure that it is hung at eye level – it may sound obvious, but it's not always done. Check there is a well-lit mirror in your bathroom. You can make the world of difference to a dark entrance hall with a strategically placed mirror. Hung over a fireplace, one often makes the ideal finishing touch to the focal point of the room. Placing a candle in front of a mirror creates an extra light source.

Making space for dining

If your house lacks a dining room, try and define a space for one instead. This may mean giving up a small area in the kitchen, living room or even the hall. To underline your message, lay the table simply but elegantly with your best matching china, glasses, cutlery and napkins, so it's clear where eating and entertaining can be enjoyed. Believe me, if you pay attention to these important details, you will add to the intrinsic value of your home.

DIAGNOSIS

At the end of this L-shaped living room was an odd area, where a sofa faced a blank wall and radiator. It felt like a waiting room. However, this property didn't have a dining room and this dead space would provide the solution. With a change of furniture, a match of ceiling lights and removal of the television, we would add an extra room to the property.

CURE

We found a table outside and cut a new tabletop from MDF. Once painted black, it was coated in gold size, a specialist adhesive, and then brushed with sheets of variegated green gold leaf before being varnished. We boxed in the radiator, which gave us a new shelf for decorative candlesticks, and hung a picture above it. As the table was so arresting, I didn't think it needed laying – a plant in the centre was enough. The ceiling light was changed to match the one in the adjoining room, and some chairs and lamps completed the transformation.

The dining end of this kitchen looked like a bit of an afterthought. It didn't feel terribly inviting. We painted the whole room a light, summery green and gave the floor a country look by laying a slab-patterned Texline floor covering. This made a huge difference and began to tie the two ends of the room together.

A mirror on the far wall reflected the kitchen, and the country dresser was improved once its contents were thinned out and rearranged. Having neutralised the room, I used the curtains to bring in colour and frame the patio outside. Lastly, some bright flowers and a new light shade finished it off.

BEFORE

AFTER

KITCHENS

The kitchen is one of the major selling points in a house, and must look as light, bright, clean and friendly as possible. No new buyer wants to sink thousands of pounds into a house immediately after they've bought it and your kitchen could cost that much to refit, so don't give the impression that's what's needed. Your buyers must be made to feel that this is a room in which they'll want to spend time, without having to spend money remodelling it.

The key elements prospective purchasers will be looking at are the kitchen units, the walls, floor and lighting. Assess these first and, if necessary, replace or update them. A lick of paint and a good clean might be all the room needs, but a more extensive revamp might be called for. Just regrouting wall tiles can immediately brighten up a tired-looking wall.

TOP 10 TIPS

1 Clean everything thoroughly. It's essential that your kitchen looks as hygienic and functional as possible.

2 Clear all inessential clutter, including last night's washing up and what's collected on the top of the units.

3 Make sure the room is as light and bright as possible. That means neutral-coloured walls with accents of colour in the room.

4 If the units look dated, consider painting them or even replacing the doors or handles altogether.

5 Check the floor. It should be spotless. If it is worn, replace it.

6 Only have new, neatly folded drying-up cloths – NOT the ones you've been drying your hands on all week!

7 If taps, cooker or hob have seen better days, replacing them is not that expensive and can give a new look to an old kitchen.

8 Finish off all minor repairs. Don't give the impression that an inexpensive new kitchen might be needed soon.

9 Get rid of any evidence of where your pets eat or sleep. Some buyers might find it unhygienic or positively offensive.

10 Baking bread, a cinnamon stick boiling on the cooker, or fresh coffee brewing adds an aroma that appeals subliminally to the buyer's senses. It gives one that feeling of 'home'.

If there are any DIY jobs left undone, now is the time to fix them. Handles and switches should be properly screwed in and cleaned; loose hinges should be tightened and squeaky doors oiled.

All your appliances should be in working order. Pay attention to minor repairs, fix handles and doors on the washing machine and oven and get a new washer for the dripping tap.

These days, people want light, bright, spacious kitchens and there are certain things you can do simply that will make yours look modern, clean and inviting. If you have used a strong wall colour, it would be wise to repaint in a much more muted tone, either subtly echoing the colour in the splashback tiles, or with a safe neutral colour. Similarly, if the units are dark, dated and intrusive, they will benefit from being painted a neutral white or cream. If they are looking really tatty, it may be worth replacing the doors or, at the very least, the handles. Ensure that doors shut properly, and check appliances. Give everything a thorough clean and banish all signs of pets from the kitchen — it immediately gives the wrong impression.

Empty all the cupboards and throw away anything that you don't need, to make room for all the junk that has accumulated on the work surfaces. Put away the toaster and kettle — keep worktops as clear as possible to increase the impression of space in the room. Just select one or two items to display — a bowl of fruit, for example, some toning clean tea towels and a vase of fresh herbs or flowers on the windowsill. And talking of windows, make sure the view out isn't one of yet more junk in the yard.

REVAMP YOUR KITCHEN FOR...

If your kitchen has lost its sparkle, it doesn't mean you have to spend a fortune buying a new one. How much you do to your kitchen depends on your budget, but with even just a lick of paint and a few well chosen accessories you can really brighten up the dullest of rooms. The key elements to consider are shown below, with approximate costings. They'll make all the difference.

UNDER £75		UNDER £150		UNDER £200	
Paint walls and woodwork	£40	Paint walls and woodwork	£40	Paint walls and woodwork	£40
Prime and paint tiles	£20	Prime and paint tiles	£20	Prime and paint tiles	£20
New kitchen towels	£10	New kitchen towels	£10	New kitchen towels	£10
		Prime and paint cupboards	£25	Prime and paint cupboards	£25
		Add new handles	£20	Add new handles	£20
				Replace worn flooring	£40
				Replace old taps	£25
				Add new curtains or blind	£20

DIY

When you're selling your house, you must attend to all those jobs that you've been meaning to tackle for months. Unfinished repairs can give the impression that there are others not so obvious to the naked eye. Finish off all minor repairs. Don't give the impression that an inexpensive kitchen might be needed soon.

DIAGNOSIS

This kitchen was a complete tip. All sorts of DIY jobs had been started, but never finished. The tiling on the walls was incomplete, the boiler door was missing and wall units had been removed, leaving behind ugly marks. Wiring was exposed in several places and the floor was covered with a tatty carpet – never a good idea in a kitchen. Emergency surgery was the only option to restore this room to one that people would want to cook in.

CURE

The first job to tackle was to tidy up the unfinished tiling. The walls were then replastered and the exposed wires covered up. Next, I mixed a beige paint with some green emulsion stainer and used this to paint the walls. We painted the unit doors white, giving them a whole new lease of life. The boiler door was found in the attic, brought downstairs and put in its rightful place. The tatty carpet was replaced with easy-to-lay, easy-to-clean vinyl flooring. Everything was thoroughly cleaned and the kitchen looked as good as new.

Declutter

As with every room, the first thing to do is remove ALL superficial clutter, including the jolly magnetic letters from the fridge door and the sheaf of notices from the pinboard. Evidence of your children and hectic social life may make you feel good, but it focuses the buyer's eyes on the wrong things.

Work space is at a premium. Clear the worktops of all but the most essential equipment so there's plenty of space for preparing food. If your kitchen table is showing signs of knife score marks, disguise them with a tablecloth or a length of colourful PVC. Make sure that the wastebin is empty. There's nothing more off-putting than rubbish spilling out all over the place. Take care of any laundry that might be piled up waiting to be washed or ironed. If you've used the tops of the wall units for storage, clear everything off them.

DIAGNOSIS

This was a very small kitchen, not helped by having practically every surface covered with stuff. Pots and pans hanging from the wall added to a general sense of chaos while scrappy old tea towels hung on the radiator, mugs and glasses on the draining board and a washing-up liquid container on the windowsill, made the kitchen look cluttered and dirty.

CURE

It was essential to create the illusion of space here. The walls were painted white, providing a striking contrast to the new blue floor tiles, maximising the sense of space. We cleared all the inessentials away – the space was exposed and it appeared as if there was enough storage capacity. The Formica tops were reinvigorated with specialist white paint and the new slatted shelves used the dead space on one wall and were less heavy and obtrusive than the old ones. The hooks below are just the place for tea towels – new ones!

Clean

Then it's time to obey my first rule of thumb: Clean, clean, and clean again. Your kitchen MUST shine. Any curtains or blinds need to be taken down and washed or cleaned. Remove all signs of animal life. If you can't house them elsewhere, wash their bedding and, of course, the pets themselves. Many buyers will find the idea of animals in the kitchen unhygienic and off-putting.

Add a bowl of fruit or a vase of flowers for a nice finishing touch.

DIAGNOSIS

Far from being the major selling point a kitchen should be, this room was a mess, which made it look grubby. Every surface had something on it. Buyers want to see the full expanse of work surface, not the colour of your sheets or how many people were drinking wine last night. The skirting boards and one of the walls were unpainted, and the overall impression was one of a gloomy corridor that led through to another door.

CURE

The washing and ironing was put away and appliance doors shut. The old towel, washing up and every inessential item (except the attractive bowl of fruit) littering the worktops were all put away. Hanging a curtain to hide the next door made the kitchen feel properly defined. The old-fashioned tongue-and-groove ceiling was transformed with white paint. We chose a pale green for the walls, which toned with the decorative tiles, and the skirting boards were painted white. The room was cleaned until it sparkled. Finally, out went the dated wood blind and in came a bright white roman blind.

Storage is a buzzword in contemporary design. It's true that you can't have enough storage space in a house. And it's one of the things that your potential buyers will definitely be on the lookout for. You may be happy living in a relaxed family home with things piled up on every surface, but they may be of a more minimalist bent and will want to be assured that their belongings will have their place. If you leave everything out, it gives the impression that the house is too small and doesn't have enough space to

put it. You can rectify this easily by the addition of some simple storage ideas. Obviously this is not the moment to build fitted cupboards but you'll find inexpensive storage systems in your local department store or DIY shop, not to mention the specialist shops that have sprung up recently. CD and video collections should be found a home off the floor. Books should be thinned out and neatly shelved. In one house I staged, we used a third bedroom specifically as a dressing room where all the jumble from the master bedroom was neatly sorted and stored. You will be able to lay your hands on all shapes and sizes of boxes to hold photos, papers and other essential bits and pieces. Canvas wardrobes, fabric shoe holders, wine racks, mobile kitchen units are only a few of the ideas that await you. If your budget won't allow the investment, then use your attic, below-stairs space and, if the worst really comes to the worst, the boot of your car!

- Alcoves on either side of the chimney breast are an ideal place for shelves.
- Open shelves in a kitchen are great for storage and don't make the room look smaller.
- Glass shelves work brilliantly in a bathroom and even across windows sometimes.
- Shelves don't have to be used for books. Ornaments can look good, too.
- Make sure all cupboard doors shut properly so they don't look as if they're literally stuffed to bursting.
- Stuff children's toys into large plastic boxes.
- Self-assembly drawers will slip neatly under a bed.

SELL IT!

It's essential that every room should have a clear function. You must make it clear to your buyer exactly what every room is for. Play up the existence of a dining room by clearing away all the children's homework and games. A third bedroom could be a bedroom, a study or a dressing room, but not all three at once. Organise some storage systems so that the principal function of the room they're in remains clearly defined. Furnish an empty room, giving it a raison d'être. If you don't want to invest in furniture before your move, ask an obliging friend if you can borrow a couple of key pieces.

Opposite: Better to hang clothes up than leave them slung over the bedroom furniture.

Left: A simple racking system can help tidy up a bathroom or kitchen.

Bottom left: All sorts of things, from clothes to toiletries, can be neatly stored in mesh boxes on a shelving system.

Bottom middle: Shoes can be a nightmare to keep tidy. A handy shoe rack makes all the difference.

Bottom right: These boxes could be used to hide away almost anything.

Units

Kitchen units can make or break the look of a kitchen. Dark wooden doors can be overpowering and dated. Melamine finishes may look as if they have seen better days. One of the easiest ways of getting a new kitchen at a fraction of the price is by replacing the doors and drawer fronts. Most replacement door manufacturers sell them in MDF, hardwood and pine. Sometimes, simply changing the handles is enough. A cheaper way is to give a fresh new look to dark or dated wooden units by painting them white. Gloss or soft sheen emulsion provides a practical, wipeable surface. First, the units must be spotlessly clean, then sand them just enough for the primer to stick. Prime then apply the topcoat. Melamine cupboards and drawers can be painted with specialist melamine paint. Is there any way you can improve the look of your worktop without replacing it? Tiles can be regrouted or painted. Wooden surfaces can be sanded, then re-oiled or resealed. Zinc and stainless steel tops can be cleaned with lemon juice to give an extra sheen. If any of the doors or drawers have come adrift, fix them back. If you don't look after something as simple as that, who knows what attention you pay to the rest of the house? Why be the one to put that doubt into a buyer's head?

AFTER

AFTER

BEFORE

This kitchen looked a bit washed out. The units were OK but didn't look their best and the room needed a thorough clean and tidy. The area below the tiles had never been finished and the gaping hole by the washing machine was an eyesore. The old floor tiles had seen better days while the floral blind was just plain fussy against the stripy wallpaper.

Instead of wallpaper, the walls were painted a deep orange while the units were freshened up with a contrasting shade of blue. We moved the washing machine and installed the boiler in its place. The blind was removed, but we needed to disguise the grim view. Cutting circles in frosted adhesive sheet, which was then stuck on the lower panes, solved the problem and added a fun aspect. Deep blue tiles were laid to provide contrast with the walls and units and the look was completed by dressing the chairs in matching blue covers.

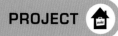
TABLE STORAGE BOX

Let a modest wooden box take on a new identity as a smart side table with invaluable hidden storage space.

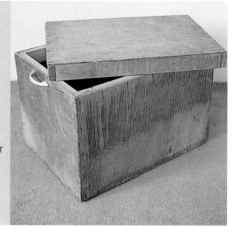

What you need

- small wooden box
- screwdriver
- ruler or tape measure
- pencil
- paper
- handsaw
- 40mm x 40mm
  (1½ x 1½in) softwood batten
- clamp or workbench
- electric drill
- dowels
- chalk
- wood glue
- hammer
- jigsaw
- plywood panels
- scissors
- panel pins
- pine board
- medium-grade sandpaper
- 2 butt hinges and screws
- bradawl
- paintbrush
- woodwash

ONE Remove and discard the box's handles, fixings and lid. Decide how high you would like the box to stand. Measure, mark and saw four appropriate lengths of batten for the legs. Place them vertically in a clamp and drill four holes in one end of each leg to hold the dowels.

TWO Make four chalk marks on the bottom of the box in each corner, where the legs will go. Drill holes in

the box base for the dowels. Squeeze wood glue into the holes in the box and legs. Insert a dowel into each hole in the legs and hammer each leg into position on the box. Do not stand the box on its legs until the glue is completely dry.

THREE Using a jigsaw, cut ply panels big enough to fit all four sides from the top of the box to the floor. First

shape a side panel by marking the position of the legs and the level of the bottom of the box. Draw a curve from the centre point to the base of one leg. Cut a paper pattern to match this curve and use to continue the curve to the other leg. Use the template on the other side panel. Repeat the process on the front and back panels.

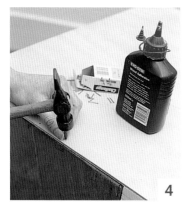

FOUR Apply glue to the side edges of one of the ply side panels. Stick it to the box and legs, securing it with panel pins at regular intervals. Repeat with the other side panel, then the front and back panels.

FIVE Cut a lid from the pine board, 3cm (1¼in) larger than the box all round. Sand smooth. Lay the box on its side next to the lid. Open the hinges and mark their positions on both the box and the lid. Make holes using a bradawl, then screw the hinges in place.

SIX Apply woodwash to the box, both inside and out. Leave to dry.

The resulting table can be used in any number of different ways and in any number of different rooms. In the bedroom it may be used to store bulky clothes such as jumpers, or as an alternative to a laundry basket. It also makes a great bedside table. In the living room, this piece will always be of use as a table and often as a

place to store magazines and newspapers. Alternatively — especially when trying to sell your home and in the absence of a toy box — use it to hide any evidence that your living room doubles as a playroom. Dual-purpose furniture is particularly useful in a property where space is limited.

Floors

Don't forget the floor. If it has taken a beating over the years, replace it with a stylish and easy-to-clean covering. A rug might brighten it up, but not near where you cook – too much will be dropped on it too quickly and you'll have to replace it.

Old, stained and worn carpets should go straight to the tip – a kitchen is no place for carpet. There is a huge choice of different floorcoverings available that are easy to lay, easy to clean and easy on the pocket. Timber floors are suitable for kitchens only if they are treated properly because bits of food and dirt will get between the joins. Wood-effect floors are easy to fit and are a smart alternative for the kitchen. Otherwise, it's worth considering linoleum (in tile or sheet form) or vinyl, both of which come in a wide variety of designs and patterns, or cork tiles.

DIAGNOSIS

This kitchen was dark, dingy and dirty, with old green carpet, dark wood units and blood red walls. The dark table and mismatched chairs didn't do the room any favours either. Things weren't helped by the unit door over the oven, which had been charred by a grease fire. Apart from a thorough clean, the room really needed a good facelift.

CURE

The old carpet was dumped in favour of a new wood-effect floor, which gave the room a cleaner, more contemporary feel. The walls looked much better painted a muted green. Dated wood units were given a new lease of life in cream and the melamine worktops were revived with a complementary shade of specialised paint. The microwave was placed on the counter by the oven, which was in such a bad state that it had to be replaced. A new table with matching chairs added to the lighter, more modern look. What could be more inviting?

AFTER

The oranges, yellows and blues in this kitchen screamed at me to put my sunglasses back on. The owner excused it by explaining that the units and work surface were there when they arrived and their choice of flooring and wall colour had been an attempt to tie the look together. He was right. Orange is a very difficult colour to work with, but, in my opinion, he'd have been better off getting rid of the lot and starting from scratch. Those colours were very dated, made the room look even smaller and took away from the view. Something drastic had to be done to play up the positive points. Where I could I wanted to work with the natural colours of the nearby seaside in this apartment. We easily replaced the garish flooring with a neutral wood laminate. Painting the walls a light sky blue made the room larger and lighter. Those nightmarish orange doors were covered with a cloud-white washable laminate that can be cut to size. Then we painted the balcony floor a golden sandy colour, which progressed naturally from the new kitchen floor and was a reminder of the beach nearby.

BEFORE

Light

Lighting can make a huge difference to the perception of a room. You may have sunshine flooding the room during the day, but what about in the evening when many prospective buyers will visit? It is important that the kitchen work surfaces, hob and oven are all lit efficiently. Fluorescent lighting strips can run under the upper kitchen cabinets to prevent the cook having to work in his or her own shadow. Alternatively, light can be directed from the ceiling, either from a track carrying spotlights or from accurately angled downlighters. It won't cost much to buy a simple tracking system that can be directed at various points. If the kitchen includes a dining area, it's a good idea to install dimmer switches so that the work areas can be faded out during a meal.

Consider replacing door panels with glass to let more light in. To soften the view from either side, you can hang sheer fabric over the door. It will let the light through and create a wonderful effect.

Above: Typical of many London basement conversions, two rooms have been knocked through to give a lighter open-plan living area and kitchen. A warm neutral colour on the walls does its usual trick of unifying the whole room and making it seem larger and lighter. With the light from the living area and the window, all that is needed is a central pendant light over the working area.

Furniture

Is the furniture in your kitchen making the room appear smaller than it is? Could a breakfast bar replace the unwieldy table? Or you could consider a drop-leaf table with some foldaway chairs that take up very little space when not being used. Lay the table with mats and glasses that tie in with the colour scheme. If you have a dresser, improve its appearance by thinning out the contents of the shelves and rearranging the items. Box in a radiator and use the top as an extra shelf.

Right: If you're short of space, consider boxing in the radiator – not only does it look more attractive, but it gives you an extra shelf.

This kitchen/dining room needed very little attention, because the colour scheme worked well with the existing furniture. The boiler had been left exposed in all its glory, but it was quite simple to have a joiner box it in using MDF. As there weren't any upper units, I felt the kitchen end of the room looked better balanced with the addition of a couple of white shelves for storage. However, the room as a whole needed bringing together so that it looked more up to date and operated better as one. To begin with, I continued the new flooring used in the living room through into the kitchen and dining area. This had the overall effect of making the whole ground floor flow together, but also making it look both smarter and more contemporary. Wood laminate is an ideal finish for a kitchen floor, being hard-wearing and easy to keep clean.

Looking at the dining end of the room, one thing was obvious. The dog and his bed would have to be found a new home in the garage outside. Apart from the fact that some buyers might be unnerved by the presence of a dog, many would be put off by its smell and by the fact that it was unhygienic having him in the kitchen. The heavy dresser wasn't doing the space any favours, but then neither did the large radiator that lurked behind it. The problem was solved with a wide radiator cover that could double as a sideboard. The wall space above was ideal for display shelves and the walls were lifted with a coat of soft sunshine yellow paint. We bought a round table for the centre of the room with some foldaway chairs, and the room presented the image of a lifestyle anyone would happily aspire to.

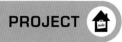
ZINC CORNER TABLE

Turn dead space in any room into a practical storage-bin-cum-table with a contemporary twist in five easy steps.

What you need
- pair of compasses and ruler
- paper and pencil
- scissors
- jigsaw and handsaw
- protective face mask
- 6mm (¼in) MDF
- paintbrush
- eggshell paint in chosen colour
- screwdriver and screws
- 10 furniture blocks
- lengths of batten
- sheet of hardboard
- perforated zinc sheeting
- 6 mirror-fixing screws with silver-coloured caps

ONE To make a quadrant template, draw and cut out a paper circle and fold it twice. Check the quadrant fits your corner, adjust, then cut out. Wearing a face mask for protection and using the template, cut three MDF quadrants. Leave one whole (base); cut a hand hole in one (lid); remove centre of the third, leaving a 4cm (1½in) border all round (top frame for lid).

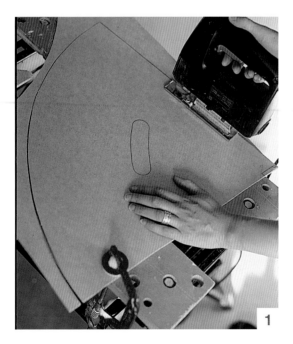

TWO Paint the lid. While it is drying, fix the base in the corner by attaching it to the walls and floor. Use two furniture blocks on each straight edge and two on the curved edge to hold the front vertical battens.

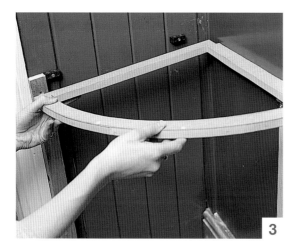

THREE Decide on the height of the table and cut two side battens to length. Screw them to the wall. Screw the remaining furniture blocks at the right height on the wall then fix the MDF top frame in position.

FOUR Cut two vertical battens to fit on the front edge of the table between the top and the base.

FIVE Cut a piece of hardboard to fit the front, adding 5cm (2in) to the height and allowing for the skirting. Cut the zinc to the same shape with an additional 2cm ($\frac{3}{4}$in) all round. Place the zinc over the hardboard and fold over the extra. Fix to the battens with mirror-fixing screws. Put the lid on top.

Walls

A coat or two of paint can magically transform your kitchen into a totally different environment. Kitchens can take a variety of colour schemes, but brightly coloured walls won't appeal to every buyer and can take attention away from the room itself. However, kitchens are the heart of the home and will respond well to cheery combinations of colours. They can be painted in an eggshell or vinyl finish, both practical paints in a kitchen where they can easily be wiped clean.

DIAGNOSIS

This was a very small kitchen and it looked very unloved and underused. The white walls made it feel like the inside of an igloo and I felt it was essential to warm the place up. The washing-up and inessential clutter on the worktops was very dispiriting, while the rubbish bin and used dishcloth did little to help matters. There wasn't much we could do about the size of the room, but we could make it more warm and inviting.

CURE

It's easy and very effective to warm up a room just by introducing some colour. Here we used a shade of blue on the walls, while the beams and tiles were painted white, to tie in with the units.

Then we needed to present the kitchen better. The first job was to clean every surface until they gleamed, and to put away clutter. The rubbish bin was removed and a bright red vegetable rack took its place.

A picture and a plant completed the injection of life into what was previously a completely cheerless room.

Sometimes when you live with a room for a long time you lose sight of the fact that the colours are dreary and depressing. Consider this room – and how much life was breathed into it with just a lick of paint.

DIAGNOSIS

It's true that grey was once the must-have colour, but in this kitchen it looked depressing and of its time. Not even the yellow coving jollied it up. The only thing to be done here was to cheer up that lifeless grey and make sure that there was something in the room to distract attention from the rather dull run of units.

CURE

Repainting the walls in a warm apricot transformed the kitchen into a much warmer, friendly place. The table was moved to the other side of the room, giving the illusion that there was a separate space within the room, clearly defined for eating in. Laying the table issues a subliminal invitation and you can combine it with delicious cooking smells – buy some half-baked bread and finish it off in the oven with some freshly made coffee on the side. Finally, the kitchen is for cooking, not watching television, so the TV was removed.

Windows

Clear window ledges of all but one or two decorative items. Clean the windows until they shine. Curtains are not always practical in a kitchen – blinds offer a neat, uncluttered look and are relatively inexpensive. They can be rolled back out of the way and they can be wipeable in the kitchen. They introduce colour and pattern, are inexpensive and can be easily replaced. You may be able to find ready-made blinds that fit, you may want to use a DIY blind kit or, of course, you can have them made to measure.

DIAGNOSIS

A kitchen needs as much light as it can possibly get – the view outside the bare window wasn't so great so we needed to let light in while making the window more attractive. The room looked old-fashioned, unloved and unlived in and reminded me of bed-sit days. What I had to do was bring it up to date and inject some life into the room.

CURE

A thin fabric blind hung at the window disguised the view, while not depriving the room of any light. A coat of fresh paint and the kitchen began to look as though it could be enjoyed again. Galvanised metal sheeting attached to the unit doors made them stylish, and a small but fashionable Shaker-style cupboard filled the dead wall space. I don't like clutter, but a few finishing touches created a fresh, natural look.

This kitchen had plenty of windows, but they felt cold and bare. Everything, including the windows, was thoroughly cleaned until it all looked spotless. I then took my lead from the kitchen door when I chose green as the accent colour and dressed the windows in green gingham curtains and blind. We painted the walls a pretty buttery cream and finished off the units with new handles. A new beech work surface gave a more completed feel to the room, which was helped by boxing in the electricity meter. My favourite addition was a dual-purpose radiator cover that doubled as a breakfast bar and brilliantly utilised what was otherwise wasted space. A green mat and green kitchen accessories all dressed in perfectly to create the feel of a real country kitchen.

BEFORE

AFTER

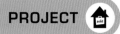
RESTYLED TABLE AND CHAIRS

Give an uninspiring set of table and chairs some pizzazz with a lick of paint, colourful fabric and a glass table top.

What you need

- table and chairs with removable seats
- protective face mask
- medium-grade sandpaper
- paintbrush, small emulsion roller and tray
- water-based primer
- emulsion paint
- ruler and tape measure
- stencil acetate
- Chinagraph pencil
- craft knife and cutting mat
- stencil brush
- clear acrylic varnish
- scissors
- fabric
- spray adhesive
- safety glass with bevelled edges for table top
- pliers and screwdriver
- thin upholstery foam for chair seats
- fabric marker pen
- staple gun

ONE Remove the seats from the chairs and, wearing a face mask for protection, sand all the wooden surfaces. Wipe clean and paint on water-based primer. When dry, paint the table and the chairs with two coats of emulsion, allowing the first coat to dry before applying the second.

2

1

TWO Measure the table top and work out the size of a square that will divide into both the table's length and width. Make a stencil by drawing parallel lines on the acetate with a Chinagraph pencil. Mark into squares and, using a craft knife, cut out alternate ones .

THREE Stencil a row of squares all around the table an equal distance apart. Stencil a second row inside them to create a chessboard effect. When the paint is dry, apply two coats of varnish to both the table and the chairs, again allowing the first coat to dry before applying the second.

FOUR Measure the area of the table inside the chequered border and cut a piece of fabric to fit. For a neater edge, allow a 1cm (³/₈in) hem. Press the fabric then spray the wrong side

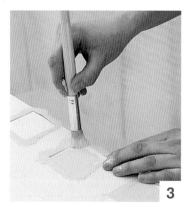

3

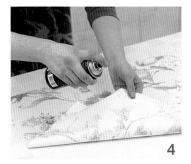

4

with adhesive before laying it carefully on the centre of the table. Place the glass on top.

FIVE Remove the old fabric and any staples or nails from the chair seats. Draw the outline of a chair seat and add 2cm (¾in) all round. Cut new pieces of foam to this size. Spray the seats with adhesive and stick the foam in place.

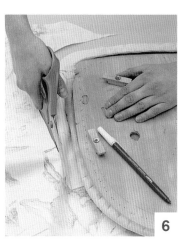

6

7

5

SIX Lay the new fabric for each chair seat, right side facing down, on a flat surface. Put the seat on top and draw around it, allowing an extra 5cm (2in) all the way round. Cut out the fabric.

SEVEN Fold in the edges of the fabric and staple to the underside of each seat. Staple first one then the opposite edge of the seat, alternating so that the fabric can be pulled to fit tightly across. Pleat the fabric carefully at the corners. Replace the seats in the chairs.

Use different fabric in the same way to create an entirely different effect. Pretty floral patterns will be at home in the country, while bright geometrics will suit a contemporary room. Plain coloured tops will claim less attention if there are other patterns working elsewhere in the room, but will help create a coordinated look.

BATHROOMS

Although the bathroom comes behind the kitchen as a selling ticket on a house, it is absolutely essential that it gets the same treatment.

Bathrooms must appear as completely clean, light and spacious as possible, and should enable buyers to imagine themselves luxuriating there. If you can't keep the room clean and tidy for yourself, then at least make the effort while you are trying to sell the house. So, on with the rubber gloves for a really good clean, remembering every surface, from skirting boards to the tiles. And put away all the cleaning products and personal belongings.

Real plants can thrive in the bathroom. They look good, can smell wonderful and don't gather dust, but remove any dead leaves and make sure that pots colour-coordinate with the room.

TOP 10 TIPS

1 No bathroom can be too clean, so use all your elbow grease to get surfaces really fresh and sparkling.

2 Declutter all surfaces. It's not necessary – or interesting – to have all your most intimate requirements on display.

3 Get rid of fitted carpets. They absorb moisture, often look tatty and smell bad.

4 Use only water-resistant floor coverings here – lino, marmoleum, vinyl, ceramic or mosaic tiles.

5 If the tiles round the bath and basin are showing their age, apply a coat of specialist tile paint to bring them up to the minute.

6 Potpourri, scented candles, and pretty fragrant soaps and oils add something sensual to the atmosphere.

7 Ensure your privacy with a new blind on the window, or install frosted glass or plastic film for that frosted 'effect'.

8 Finish off all DIY jobs and, if necessary, install additional lighting and storage.

9 Purchase a new shower curtain, toilet seat, and fresh, coordinating towels.

10 Badly stained or soiled grout should be cleaned or recoloured.

The things potential purchasers will be assessing are the bathroom suite, the walls, flooring and lighting. If you can't afford a new suite, clean the existing one until it sparkles, get rid of limescale and touch up enamel chips with specialist paint.

When you're selling your house, you must attend to all those jobs that you've been meaning to tackle for months. If there is any DIY you've never quite got round to, like replacing the washers on the dripping tap, the broken loo seat or towel rail, fix them. Then polish up all the chrome. Is the shower curtain hanging sleekly on all its hooks or looking forlorn and water-marked? If it's seen better days splash out on a new one, making sure you hang it properly.

Invest in a new lavatory seat and replace carpet with vinyl, lineoleum or ceramic tiles. Consider painting the walls a pale colour, so that the room appears light and clean.

I am very keen on using mirrors whenever possible and they are essential in the bathroom. They create the impression of extra space and light. Select the frames to suit the style of your room.

REVAMP YOUR BATHROOM FOR...

A new bathroom suite needn't cost the earth, but there are also cheaper alternatives. New taps, shower curtains, blinds and flooring will all brighten and freshen up the room. A new lavatory seat and a large mirror will also work wonders. Finally, if the walls are painted, freshen them up with a new coat of paint.

UNDER £75	UNDER £150	UNDER £250
Paint walls and woodwork £40	Paint walls and woodwork £40	Paint walls and woodwork £40
Clean tiles and grout work with grout revive £8	Clean tiles and grout work with grout revive £8	Clean tiles and grout work with grout revive £8
Buy new mat set £8	Replace flooring £30	Replace flooring £30
Replace shower curtain £10	Replace shower curtain £10	Replace shower curtain £10
	Buy new accessories (towel rail, lavatory seat, etc.) £25	Buy new accessories (towel rail, lavatory seat, etc.) £25
	Add new bathroom towels £25	Add new bathroom towels £25
		Replace old taps £30
		Add a blind or install frosted glass £30
		Improve lighting e.g. spotlights £40

Declutter and clean

And I do mean clean! You cannot apply too much elbow grease to the bath, basin and lavatory. Clean them for all you are worth, right down to the hairs that are caught in the plug hole. Clean the grouting between the tiles and remove any limescale from them. If any tiles are loose or missing, splash out on a small tub of tile cement and stick them back in place.

Remove all the clutter, including your well-used toothbrush and squashed-up toothpaste tube. Nobody wants to know what deodorant you use or any other details of your ablutions – get rid of what you can and hide the rest in a medicine cabinet on the wall. Old dog-ends of soap stuck to the side of the basin are a grim sight. Bin them and replace with a deliciously smelly new substitute. The childen's bathtime might be precious, but not many buyer's hearts will be lifted by the sight of brightly coloured plastic toys littering what might one day be their bathroom. Clear them away.

BEFORE

AFTER

Tiles

Tiles provide a hygienic, hard-wearing surface that is ideal for bathrooms. However, to look their best, they must be kept spotless. If cleaning them isn't enough to spruce up the room, there are a number of ways to improve their look without necessarily going to the trouble of replacing them.

First inspect the grouting. If it has been painted, you may want to change the colour by using specialist grout-painting pens. Always do a test area first and see how it reacts over a couple of weeks. Alternatively, get rid of any discoloured or cracked areas by carefully regrouting. This will involve removing the existing grout, then applying and levelling new grout (specialist tools are available in DIY shops for both these jobs). Use a damp cloth to wipe off the excess. It may also be necessary to reseal the join between the tiles and the bathtub by cutting out the old sealant and applying new.

If the tiles themselves are stained, dated, the wrong colour or just plain ugly, there are a number of specialist tile paints that will instantly transform them. Alternatively, you may want to give them a new lease of life by sticking on small ceramic or vinyl appliqués, such as ceramic shells. Or you can repaint them with a specialist tile primer and paint — a very simple but effective cure.

Walls

A coat of paint can transform your bathroom into a totally different environment. Prospective buyers won't be taken with any inventive colour schemes, so consider painting the walls a pale colour, a soft blue or a primrose yellow, so that the room appears light, clean, intimate and relaxing. Eggshell or vinyl finish paints are ideal in a bathroom because they are waterproof.

DIAGNOSIS

This bathroom badly needed rescuing from a time-warp. The original wallpaper, no doubt fashionable when it was put up twenty years earlier, looked hopelessly out of date, while the carpet covered even the side of the bath! I couldn't do anything about the yellow fittings, but I could minimise their impact by changing what was round them and calming down the walls.

CURE

The wallpaper was painted over in a shade that complemented the bathroom suite, and the wooden window frame was glossed over in white. I replaced the carpet with self-adhesive floor tiles to give a much slicker finish to the room. Clean, carefully folded towels and a fresh bar of soap were the only other accessories needed to kickstart this bathroom into the twenty-first century. One tip: I should have left the lavatory seat down. It looks so much better and in feng shui terms you risk flushing energy and money away.

Windows

Look at the treatment of the windows and give window frames a lick of paint to freshen them up if necessary. Check the windows for ease of opening and oil the hinges if they're sticking. Keep window ledges clear of all clutter and clean the windows until they shine. Curtains are not always practical in a bathroom. Stick-on plastic etching can be an effective way of maintaining privacy while admitting light, while blinds are relatively inexpensive and offer a neat uncluttered look. Make sure they are kept clean and operational. They can be rolled back out of the way, are available in waterproof materials and they can introduce colour and patterns.

DIAGNOSIS

What was a pet rat doing in the bathroom? It gave the impression that the room was unhygienic. A window ledge was covered with bits and pieces, while the window itself needed dressing. The floral tiles and wallpaper had a dizzying effect, bringing the walls in and making the room seem very small. The whole room needed a thorough clean and tidy.

CURE

Obviously the first thing to go was the rat, swiftly followed by the carpet, which we replaced with a wood flooring in French rustic oak. The window wasn't a particularly attractive feature, so we bought a simple Roman blind, which hid it while still admitting as much light as possible. I wanted to break up the large expanse of wall above the tiling and chose a mirror to increase the amount of light in the room. We painted the wallpaper a warm apricot, which toned with the tiles, and then gave the room a thorough clean. What a difference!

Lighting and mirrors

Bathroom lighting is strictly regulated to avoid water coming into contact with it. The only switch acceptable in the room is a pull cord. Otherwise switches should be mounted outside the room. In addition to overhead lighting there should be lighting above or on either side of the mirror, and the basin/shaving area might have a shaving light socket. Dimmer switches enable you to change the mood in your bathroom, creating a more soothing atmosphere in the evenings. Fluorescent lights are particularly unflattering.

To create an intimate, relaxing mood, have scented candles around the bath. Their light will also have the advantage of disguising any real eyesores. But that may not be to everyone's taste, so make sure that the existing lights are strong enough to light the room properly.

Mirrors are often a clever way of both making a small room look bigger and enhancing the available light. Rather than having a tiny mirror over the basin, perhaps it would benefit the room to replace it with something bigger.

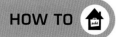

USE PLANTS DECORATIVELY

Plants and flowers can add life, colour and contrast to a room, but only if they are healthy and displayed well. Unless you are blessed with green fingers, it is wise to choose plants that will withstand almost any amount of neglect. Take advice from the local garden centre. When choosing a plant, make sure that it looks healthy, that roots are not coming out of the pot's drainage holes and that there is no moss or slime on the compost.

Caring for plants

Houseplants come in all shapes and sizes to suit almost any situation. The rules of thumb when caring for indoor plants are: put them where they will thrive best, not only where they look best; water and feed them according to instructions; treat any disease or pest the moment you spot it; avoid extremes of cold and heat; trim off dead flowers and leaves; if a plant begins to look as if it is suffering, ask yourself why it is suffering and remedy it. Find out what conditions your plants experience in the wild and try to imitate them as closely as possible in terms of compost, light, temperature and water.

Choosing containers

There is no limit to the type of containers suitable for houseplants. There is no reason why you can't use decorative tins, seaside buckets, teapots, glass containers or even an old butler's sink. The most common container of course is the tried-and-tested terracotta pot, which goes well with any plant and allows moisture to evaporate through its sides. Such pots can be used alone or placed inside a cache-pot whose design suits the décor better. Groups of plants can make an attractive feature or focal point in a room. They may be freestanding, or smaller arrangements will fit into terrariums, bottle gardens or a trough. Window boxes do not have to be restricted to the outside of the house. If there's no sill or they are in danger of falling, try bringing them inside. They may be ideal for growing herbs or small flowering border plants.

Use your imagination to find ways of using plants to enhance a space, be it dramatic, exotic, soothing or just plain welcoming. Remember, a few well chosen, well cared-for plants are an asset to any décor; an overgrown jungle is a definite liability.

What plant goes where?

Small, bushy flowering pot plants such as chrysanthemums, azaleas or cyclamen make good seasonal centrepieces for tables, and will also sit happily on a mantelpiece or windowsill. They can be difficult to keep alive after they have flowered and are often transplanted into the garden. Trailing plants such as the spider plant, sweetheart plant, wandering Jew or devil's ivy can sit on a plant stand, shelf or wall bracket and cascade downwards. If placed near a window, they can be used to hide an unappealing view. The important thing to remember is that just because they're out of easy reach, they still need the same attention as any other plant or they will become leggy and miserable. Exotic palms make grand architectural statements. They suit both a modern minimalist environment and a busier more traditional room where they

can be combined with other plants in an impressive display. They will live particularly happily in living or dining rooms where the temperature remains reasonably constant.

If you want to put greenery into your bathroom, try one of the ferns. They love a warm humid environment so if the bathroom doesn't steam up often, make sure you spray them regularly. Kitchens are generally not a great home for plants because of the fluctuating temperature. But if you insist, it's best to go for the real death-defying specimens such as peace lilies, sweetheart plants, mother-in-law's tongues, devil's ivy or umbrella plants. If you just want something small on the window ledge, try growing your own herbs.

Flooring

Double check the flooring. Curling linoleum is a turn-off and it is well worthwhile replacing it – vinyl and linoleum are always good flooring solutions, but you might also consider rubber (in tile or sheet form). They are all hard-wearing, waterproof and easy to clean.

Carpet soaks up water, with the result that it never looks its best and very often smells. There are lots of fabulous tiles that you could use instead, including sheets of beautiful mosaic.

Timber floors are not recommended for bathrooms – there is a danger that water may seep through and rot the wood.

DIAGNOSIS

This bathroom looked dirty and uncared for – with grubby old flooring and a ghastly bathmat. If it looks like a tip, your bathroom won't help you sell your house. There's no need to have all that junk on the floor, or on the cistern, while the dark walls do nothing to give the impression of cleanliness.

CURE

All it took was a lick of lilac paint for this dreary bathroom to be transformed into somewhere funky and contemporary. The bathmat hit the dustbin, while the tired old flooring was replaced with some stylish grey tiles that blend in with the new colour scheme and complete a modern look. The look was completed with the clean white tiles that ran along the walls by the basin and toilet. Rather than an ugly bathroom cabinet, we put up glass shelves, which hardly intrude on the room and provide storage for a select number of things.

Accessories

Now you're ready to dress the room, neatly positioning a few well-chosen accessories. Potpourri and scented candles can help add a suggestion of other, more sensuous possibilities.

A lot of plants thrive in the humid atmosphere of a bathroom. Using a healthy, shiny-leaved one is a very effective way of making a dramatic statement. However, keeping several old ferns with browning leaves is not. If they don't cut it, get rid of them and buy something new.

Other stylish and economical finishing touches include: towels, which should look luxurious, neatly folded and matching; bathmat — get rid of that miserable damp rag that's seen too many wet feet and buy a new one as a present to yourself; and toilet paper — look generous with it and make sure it's not tucked away behind the lavatory where it can't be seen or reached. And finally — especially to all you men — leave the loo seat firmly down: apart from anything else, in feng shui terms, this will prevent you losing wealth. And, after all, that's what all this is about.

BEDROOMS

When staging your house for sale, remember the importance of the master bedroom. It's the most personal space in the house and you should consider spending a good deal of your budget to make the most of it. A buyer won't want a room that leaves their nerves jangling from unexpected combinations of bright colours, nor one that gives the impression of being a storeroom with a bed in a corner. Once again, it's a question of clearing out all that clutter to maximise the space so the room looks as large as possible.

Present the room in a way that will appeal to the greatest number of people. Unattractive wall colours and carpets should be replaced with warm, neutral shades where necessary, while highlighting an unusual feature can give a room a whole new personality.

TOP 10 TIPS

1 Walls should be painted a warm, neutral colour, such as a soft peach, apricot or apple green. Strong colours and patterns may overwhelm a buyer and put them off.

2 Replace a worn carpet with a new one or, if the floorboards are in good condition, sand and stain them and invest in a couple of accent rugs.

3 Clear all clutter. But this is the one room where it is all right to display a few well-chosen personal photos.

4 Arrange the furniture so the room appears at its most spacious and maximum light comes through the window.

5 Make a feature of a window with a view, framing it with a pair of attractive colour-coordinated curtains.

6 Buy a set of new bedlinen or make sure the linen that you have is clean and ironed properly to give the impression that you care for your home.

7 If you're transforming a former junk room into a second bedroom and require a bed, beg, borrow or even hire one until your sale is achieved.

8 Complete the whole transformation with the addition of potpourri, scented candles or essential oils – one scent per room, please.

9 However much you love your pets, remove them from the room. You may not notice their smell, but it can be extremely off-putting to potential buyers.

10 Check your lighting. Make sure the shades are clean, the bulbs work, and that the best features are highlighted.

Without exception, a bedroom must always be inviting, offering itself as a place of retreat with a soothing, peaceful atmosphere within. By day, the room should look fresh, light and bright. Strident colours, patterns and floral prints on the walls are out. They make the room look smaller and may put off some buyers altogether.

If you're showing your room in the evening, make sure your lighting is effective. Directed right, it can help disguise the worst features by highlighting the best ones. Bedside lights are often more effective than a ceiling light. Check that all the lampshades are clean and the light bulbs are all working. Candles always give a flattering light and provide an enticing, romantic atmosphere.

And don't forget to colour coordinate the accessories to give a fresh, up-to-date look. Make sure those buyers leave, wanting to come back soon.

REVAMP YOUR BEDROOM FOR...

Evaluate the windows in the bedroom - you need privacy, peace and quiet. Do the curtains do the trick? Consider repainting or rewallpapering the walls, and renew the carpet if necessary. New bed linen and accessories will freshen the room up, as will new wardrobe doors.

UNDER £50		UNDER £100		UNDER £200	
Paint walls and woodwork	£20	Paint walls and woodwork	£20	Paint walls and woodwork	£20
Add cushions	£25	Add some cushions	£25	Add some cushions	£25
		Replace curtains	£30	Replace curtains	£30
		Replace old handles	£20	Replace old handles	£20
				Improve lighting	£30
				Add a new rug	£20
				Replace old bed linen	£50

Colour schemes

Having cleared the room, look at it objectively. What will the colours say to another person? Dominant colours distract from other features in the room. It's always sensible to repaint them. Take your colour scheme from something in the room, such as a picture or the curtains, and plan your accents from that. It only takes a couple of pots of paint to turn an idiosyncratic choice of wallpaper into something more neutral. And you can take the chill off the coldest room by painting the walls a more friendly colour.

DIAGNOSIS

What a depressing room! A bedroom should always be presented as calm and peaceful. The wall colour made the room feel claustrophobic, as did the painting. A window looked out onto a brick wall, adding to the sombre atmosphere, though a curtain or blind would only make things worse. Otherwise, the place needed a thoroughly good clean and tidy.

CURE

I chose a delicate primrose yellow for the walls with white woodwork, making the room seem twice the size and much lighter. Rather than darken the room with curtains or blinds, I masked out a narrow outline round the edge of each pane and sprayed the rest with etch spray. An electrician fixed up a weatherproof lamp outside to shine in through the window. Light streamed in, glare was reduced and privacy maintained by the etch effect. New bedlinen and a new grey cushion helped transform the room into a peaceful haven.

Colour schemes (continued)

Strong colours and garish patterns aren't to everyone's taste, while colour clashes are another horror. It's cheaper to paint the walls than to change the carpet, so if you have mismatched colours in the room alter them to something more harmonious.

DIAGNOSIS

This bedroom had me again screaming in horror at the colour of the walls, and the blue cupboards didn't go with anything. The windows were ineffectively draped and the pictures over the bed distracted the eye. A rumpled bed, a television and the chair – they all had to go. I had to realise the potential of a truly luxurious place of rest.

CURE

Taking my cue from the cupboards, I picked a blue-and-cream colour scheme for the room, which immediately looked bigger. The windows were a focal point, but were not exploited to their full potential. We rehung the curtains and instantly improved the appearance of the bay. I removed the ugly chair and television, replacing them with a stunning blue-and-white vase. A large elephant picture replaced the three smaller ones over the bed, reinforcing the slightly oriental feel to the room. The owner was thrilled with the result.

DIAGNOSIS

This bedroom was hideous. The camouflage décor was decidedly off-putting, not to mention the fact that the bed was in pieces against the wall. Once we had emptied it, I could see where to begin if a buyer was to see the potential of the room.

CURE

The first job was to paint over those walls. I decided on a seaside theme, so the walls were painted blue and I used accessories such as a lifebelt and some bright plastic buckets on one shelf and tiny coloured beach huts on another. The owner finally built the bed and put it next to the wall. A jaunty red-striped duvet cover chimed with the carpet and curtains, both of which were already in the room but barely noticeable under the chaos. As a nod to the family's army connections, I allowed an orderly row of toy soldiers back onto a shelf, but now they looked a little upgraded given their new surroundings. I decided to take the computer from the living room and give it pride of place in a corner. The room now clearly gave the message that it could be used as a small second bedroom or even as an office.

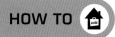
MAKE THE MOST OF LIGHTING

Light and shade will be crucial components in the design of your home. Used cleverly they can highlight and disguise good and bad features. Lighting is often overlooked in the planning of a room, but remember it can change the atmosphere at the flick of a switch. The right lighting can bring a room alive or calm it down. It can be dramatic, soothing, romantic or just plain functional. It is up to you to set the tone.

Left: Cool white blinds and thin muslin hangings at the windows provide privacy, but don't obstruct the light flow.

natural lighting

Watch the direction of sunlight entering each room and see how its effect changes throughout the day. Your choice of colours and arrangement of furniture should take this into account. Kitchens and living rooms benefit from having as much light as possible encouraged into the room. Clean the windows. Pull back curtains so they don't obstruct the light flow. Use light colours on the walls and furniture. In darker rooms, use gloss on the woodwork and hang mirrors to reflect more natural light into the space.

artificial lighting

When planning the lighting in a room, you must think about the layout of the room, how it is used, the furniture and the kinds of light that will suit the style of the room. Remember to take safety into account. You don't want accidents arising from badly lit kitchens or bathrooms, or from people tripping over stray flexes.

LIGHTING TYPES

The most effective, easy way to transform a room is by changing the lighting. Dimmer switches give more flexibility still.

● Ambient lighting

Every room needs ambient or background lighting. Steer clear of central pendant lights because they can cast a rather bleak unfriendly atmosphere. Ceiling downlighters or spotlights can be angled for the right effect and, if on a dimmer, can produce a practical bright light by day and a more soothing intimate mood by night. If they are wired in separate circuits, you can dim one area of a room and illuminate another, governing the focus of the evening. For example, you may want to forget about the kitchen and concentrate on the dining table then, after the meal, shift attention towards the sitting area without having to be reminded of the washing up. A different mood can be established by introducing subtle shadows. Table lights, standard lamps and wall lights can all be used to this effect. Wall lights or uplighters will wash the walls in a softer, more flattering glow.

● Task lighting

You will need concentrated areas of light on work surfaces, desks, reading or sewing chairs. There are all sorts of spotlights on the market ideal for task lighting. You may prefer a desk lamp or a standard spotlight to light wherever you are working. Kitchen worktops can be lit by angled downlighters, halogen spotlights on tracks or fluorescent lights under the upper wall cabinets. Bathroom mirrors will need good lighting, too, and almost everyone needs a good bedside light.

● Dramatic lighting

You may also want lights to accentuate specific features in a room. Pictures, ornaments, plants or particular architectural features can all benefit from being in the spotlight. Lastly, flickering candles and firelight will completely change the ambience of the room. They convey a warmth, romanticism and sense of relaxation unlike any other.

Declutter

Bedrooms can very quickly become dumping grounds for all sorts of things. Children's rooms, especially, are bound to be full of everything under the sun, and your children will just have to be persuaded to pack it all up for the time being. Put away any clothes you've left lying around, and if you share the room with your pets, now's the time to find them a new sleeping space.

DIAGNOSIS

Where to begin? This master bedroom had mysteriously fallen into the hands of a teenage boy, who had turned it into a pit. To present one of the principal rooms of a house like this is madness. There wasn't an inch of space to be seen and we could barely get into the room. There was serious work to be done here.

CURE

The boy and his clutter were relocated to a secondary bedroom.

I could then start from scratch and turn the room into somewhere someone might want to spend the night. Wallpapering giant posters onto the walls may have seemed a good idea at the time, but it was extremely hard work to get them off again. Having finally succeeded, the walls were ready to be lined, then painted a soft country beige. Those were the principal things that contributed to the transformation of the room. Then it was a question of finding the right furniture in the rest of the house and dressing the room so that it looked elegant and spacious. New bedlinen and curtains made the room much fresher and more inviting.

Another teenager's room, although not quite as bad as the previous one. Although everything was in order, the room was over-crowded and had some particularly unattractive spray paintings on the wall. Once we'd thinned out the clutter, a coat of primer was applied to the walls so that the paintings wouldn't show under the new paint colour I'd planned.

To tie in with the blue carpet and curtains, we painted the walls a restful shade of pale green, which looked much better. A work area was created in an alcove, all the surfaces were cleared and clothes put away so that the room and its potential could be seen clearly.

BEFORE

AFTER

Create a focus

It's important to create a focal point in the room. If a window is the only option, then ensure it looks it best by dressing it with suitable curtains or blinds. If there's a fireplace, make sure it suits the period of the house. If it's boxed in then have the courage to reinstate it. Grates and surrounds can be found at architectural salvage yards for reasonable prices. Use a fire or candles in the grate, or add a firescreen or a dried flower arrangement to smarten it up. Hanging a mirror above the mantelpiece will increase the sense of space and light in the room, or it's the perfect place to hang a favourite picture.

DIAGNOSIS

It didn't need a house doctor to see what was wrong with this room. It was empty! Because there was no furniture to act as a focus and distract the eye, the yellow décor was horribly overpowering. It was essential to define the purpose of the room to help viewers to imagine themselves living there. Besides, a second bedroom can only add value to a house.

CURE

Since there was only one other bedroom in the house we decided to present this room as a second bedroom. The wardrobes were already there, but the obvious thing missing was the bed. We were concerned with selling the house and not getting a good night's sleep so we bought one from a second-hand shop. Once we'd made it up with fresh new bed linen, nobody would spot the difference. Inexpensive bedside tables and lights and four new pictures were the finishing touches to the room, which now had focus and purpose.

The diagnosis was straightforward enough: the bedroom had never been finished. There was a marked air of general neglect and the room left too many question marks in a viewer's mind. Leaking roof? Damp? The window and fireplace were prime candidates for making into focal points. And as for the unpleasant-looking bedding and paper light shade, they had to be replaced before an injection of life began and the room given focus.

CURE

After preparing the wall, we painted it a soft apple green. The paper lantern was replaced by a toning green shade, and, using the bedspread as the basis for other colours, I chose scatter cushions and a throw to disguise the old blue sofa. The window frame was treated and painted and the split-cane blind replaced with a lighter fabric one, which disguised the uninspiring view, but let lots of light. I turned the bed to face the fireplace, and added a chest of drawers and bookshelf to suggest the room was lived in and had storage space.

Furniture

Look at the way the furniture is arranged. Minimise the number of pieces or the bedroom will seem cramped. Clear the top of the wardrobe of all junk and consider if it would be better placed against another wall.

Double check that your bed is in the best position it could be. Make sure that there's access to it from both sides and, if possible, that it faces towards the window, particularly if there's a good view. And see that it isn't blocking the door. If, for some reason, the bed base is resting on the floor, attach its legs or raise it on bricks hidden by a valance. Otherwise it looks too much like a student pad. A new bedspread or duvet can do wonders for brightening up the room too, particularly if combined with some colourful cushions.

DIAGNOSIS

What a mishmash of furniture there was in this room, including the ironing board. The place was full of clutter and horribly untidy. The wallpaper and curtains were busy and distracting and didn't go well with the crumpled, stripey duvet cover. I wanted to restore the room to its rightful position as a secondary bedroom and give it a completely new look.

CURE

I decided on a new blue colour scheme taken from the existing curtains and carpet. The walls were painted a cool blue and new bedlinen set off by a toning throw. We disguised the radiator using MDF to build a cover – slashed to let the heat out – with a reasonable-sized storage chest in front of it. For the top of the chest, I covered a foam seat pad with blue fabric and added contrasting cushions. We relocated the old dressing table and added two large floor cushions for comfort and relaxation. What an improvement!

If you haven't got a bedside table, either buy one cheaply (an MDF flat pack with a pretty table cover is easy and inexpensive), or remove your alarm clock and glass of water from the floor. Make sure that your wardrobe and chest of drawers shut properly, otherwise the room will look untidy, destroying the tranquillity you are striving to convey.

This master bedroom needed very little doing to it, but looked rather empty. It was very pretty and private with a great view into the garden, but the bed was very awkwardly positioned, 'like a daybed gone wrong', so we turned it to face into the room. This left space for the rest of the furniture to be repositioned in a way that made the room look bigger. The dressing table looked better in front of the window where it was framed by some very pretty new curtains in sheer fabric. All that remained was to work with what was already there, rehanging pictures more carefully and adding a useful small shelf unit. Lastly, we made the bed with new bedlinen and added a couple of toning cushions. Those few touches were enough to change a friendly but bare-looking bedroom into a tranquil sanctuary that no one could resist.

BEFORE

AFTER

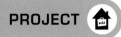
UPDATED CHEST OF DRAWERS

Take years off a plain chest of drawers with a facelift that brings it winging its way into the 21st century.

What you need

- chest of drawers
- screwdriver
- tape measure and pencil
- saw or jigsaw
- 10mm (⅜in) MDF
- protective face mask
- panel pins and hammer
- PVA glue
- 15mm (⅝in) pine board
- 4 legs (in kit form)
- medium-grade sandpaper
- paintbrushes
- 2 shades of vinyl matt emulsion paint
- liquid beeswax and soft cloths
- clear resin knobs

1

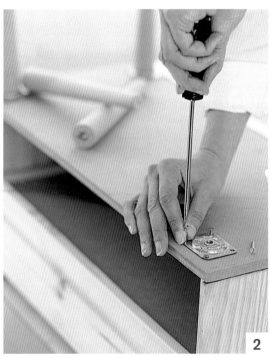

2

ONE Remove the handles from the drawers. Turn the chest upside down and measure its length and breadth. Wearing a face mask for protection, cut a piece of MDF, to fit and secure to the base of the chest using panel pins 30mm (1¼in) apart. To fill out the recessed panel, measure its width and height, adding 10mm (⅜in) to cover the new MDF. Cut the pine to measure and stick in place with PVA glue.

TWO Screw securing plates on the MDF base, 15mm (⅝in) from each corner. Screw in the new legs.

THREE Remove the drawers. Sand them and the chest before painting with two coats of emulsion, using the darker shade for the body of the chest and alternating it with the lighter shade on the drawer fronts. When the paint is dry, wax the entire surface with beeswax. Using a soft cloth, buff till it gleams. Add the new knobs to complete the look.

3

Bedroom/office/study

If a bedroom has to double as an office, workroom or study, it's a good idea to build in some furniture that can be used as desk and storage. There are so many attractive storage boxes and filing systems around that there's no excuse for untidiness.

DIAGNOSIS

This bedroom doubled as an office, but clutter on such a grand scale is far from conducive to a good night's sleep or coherent thought. The untidy shelves, mismatch of pictures on the walls and wilting plant were a real turn-off to potential buyers. Before anything was done to this room, it had to be thoroughly cleared and cleaned.

CURE

The lifeless wall colour was changed to a smart blue, which immediately lifted the room and brought it bang up to date. The deliberate absence of pictures contrasted strongly with its previous incarnation and now promoted a feeling of calm. The old table was replaced with a built-in desk unit with a long shelf above it. The stripped wooden floor has a strong finish and is cheaper than recarpeting. The dying plant was removed and with attractive new linen on the bed the room had been transformed on a relatively small budget.

I decided to turn this second bedroom-cum-office into a definitive office. All the clutter was cleared and then it was time to get to work on the room itself. It was just a case of making the room look less busy by eliminating the wallpaper under a coat of restful blue paint toning with the existing curtains and carpet. A general tidy of the desk and chest of drawers, and the admittance of a small bookcase with carefully arranged books immediately gave the impression of an efficient workplace. Should the work become too tiring, there was always the daybed. I felt this looked better with a new cover in a muted orange. The jolly blue scatter cushions tied the whole thing in with the rest of the room. Just in case it looked too sterile, I added some plants, fresh flowers and a couple of ornaments for interest.

BEFORE

AFTER

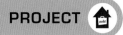
HANDY WORK SPACE

Some clever planning is all that is needed to convert a small space into a functional workstation.

inside a wardrobe

What you need

- wooden wardrobe
- pencil and ruler
- screwdriver, wood screws and small chipboard screws
- 8 small right-angled brackets
- handsaw
- 2.4m (2½yd) of 17 x 25mm (1⅟₁₆ x 1in) softwood batten
- 2 shelves of 18mm (1⅟₁₆in) MDF cut to fit wardrobe
- electric drill and assorted drill bits
- 2.4m (2½yd) of 6 x 18mm (¼ x 1⅟₁₆in) softwood batten
- large bulldog clips
- wastepaper bin
- document rack
- paintbrush
- eggshell paint
- 7 magazine files
- 12mm (½in) M6 roofing bolts
- nuts and bolts
- keyboard drawer
- noticeboard
- double-sided mirror pads
- printer tidy
- foldaway stool

ONE Use right-angled brackets and thick battening to make two shelf supports inside the wardrobe, one 38cm (15in) from the top, the other at a comfortable desk height. Slide in the shelves. Drill a hole in the side/back of the wardrobe for cables to exit.

TWO Cut six thin battens, 36cm (14¼in) long. Drill a hole at each end. In four, drill holes where the bulldog clips will sit. In the centre of one, drill two holes 3cm (1¼in) apart for a wastepaper bin. In the last, drill holes to match the pre-drilled holes on the document rack.

THREE Paint the battens and the fronts of the magazine files. Put the files on the top shelf when dry.

FOUR Use roofing bolts to attach the bulldog clips and document rack to their battens. Drill holes in the bin 3cm (1¼in) apart close to the top of the bin. Attach it to its batten using nuts and bolts. Screw the battens onto the door.

1

FIVE Fit the keyboard drawer beneath the desk shelf, following the manufacturer's instructions. Fix the noticeboard above the bulldog clips using mirror pads.

SIX Put your computer equipment in place and store a foldaway stool in the cupboard.

5

under the stairs

The space underneath stairs is often under-utilised. It may be ideal for converting into a compact office. A table, a chair and some innovative storage systems are all that is needed. Look at the space carefully and make sure every bit is used efficiently, right down to the areas under the highest and lowest steps. Think about the kind of lighting that will best illuminate the area. If you find it hard to keep your paperwork under control or want a degree of privacy, consider adding doors or a screen to shut the area off from view.

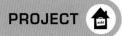
FABRIC-COVERED SCREEN

Transform a screen that has seen better days into a feature that will add a touch of class to any room.

What you need

- panelled screen
- tailor's chalk
- scissors
- fabric and matching thread
- tape measure
- iron-on hemming
- pins and safety pins
- staple gun
- rope (for handles)
- braid
- hammer and brass upholstery nails
- screwdrivers and screws
- hinges and small screw-in brass castors
- pictures for framing

ONE Separate and strip the screen's panels. Cut two contrasting fabric pieces per panel, each 1.5cm (⅝in) larger all round than the panel. Make sure any patterns match across the panels and that motifs are centred.

Frame: Cut a 35cm (14in) fabric square with a 23cm (9in) square 'window'. Cut 1cm (⅜in) diagonals at the 'window' corners.

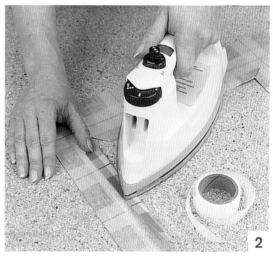

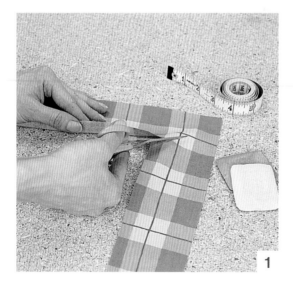

TWO Turn a 1.5cm (⅝in) hem round the 'window' and fix with iron-on hemming. Press a 1.5cm (⅝in) hem round the outside edges. Fix one (top edge) with hemming.

Pocket: Cut a 36 x 26cm (14¼ x 10¼in) rectangle of fabric and hem. Stitch along one long edge (opening) to strengthen. Machine stitch required number of pockets and frames onto the fabric panels, leaving top edges open.

THREE Turn under the edges of the large fabric pieces before stapling to the panels. Stretch the fabric outwards from the centre for a smooth fit.

FOUR Handles: Cut two 4 x 20cm (1½ x 8in) strips of fabric. Fold in half lengthways, right sides facing. Sew a 5cm (2in) seam down the longer side. Turn the right side out. Pull an 18cm (7in) length of rope through each 'tube', using a safety pin to help.

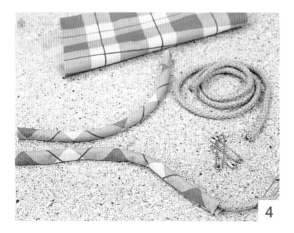

FIVE Fix braid to cover the edges, evenly spacing the nails. Start from the midpoint on the bottom edge of each panel. Turn in the raw ends of the handles, attach them to the outside edges of the outside panels. Lay the panels flat. Attach hinges and castors. Slide pictures into the fabric frames.

Box rooms

A lot of people have a valuable asset in their houses that is completely wasted – a box room, usually used for piling boxes of junk and everything under the sun into. This is madness when houses cost as much as they do – it will add value to your house only if you present it well. Clear it out, freshen it up and let the buyer see its potential.

This turret room contained a broken bed, an old mattress and boxes storing cutlery and glasses. An open-top tank dripped in a corner. Abandoning a room like this is the same as putting money on the table, then walking away from it. No matter how small a box room is, you can always make it look presentable. Drastic action was required. Adding a banister for safety and repairing the door made the approach more welcoming. We hid the tank with MDF doors. A warm blue and yellow colour scheme countered the low temperature and a new blind and light fitting were added. With new bedlinen that toned with the walls, the room was presented in a new light.

It could now be a child's room, an au pair's room, a playroom, or just a getaway.

This was another wasted box room. Stuffed with a bed the owner had yet to finish making, the laundry and the ironing board, it looked more like an enormous cupboard. It is essential to make every room work towards getting that sale. So we finished it by tidying away the clutter, which was helped by boxing in the space under the bed to create a storage area. It was now on its way to becoming a single room. Fixing the doors to the cupboard under the bed gave the room a cleaner finish. Then the walls were painted a discreet blush pink. All that was needed was a new duvet to give it a bit of class plus some Chinese symbols on the wall, inspired by the new bedding.

ACCESSORIES

The bedroom is the one room where, when selling your house, I allow personal photographs. So invest in some pretty frames and use them on your bedside table or mantel. It's worth investing in new bedlinen, which will look great and reinforce the impression that this is a house you've loved and taken care of. If you don't want the added expense, at least make sure that what you have is clean and ironed. Finally, add a few finishing touches — perhaps cushions at the head of the bed or a throw, neatly folded at the foot; scented candles, potpourri or fresh flowers will add to the atmosphere, too.

This bedroom needed work. Nobody in their right mind would sleep in there. The walls were a hideous pea green and the duvet was peculiarly masculine. The 'furniture' consisted of a broken mirror and an unattractive old-fashioned chair. It looked more like a monk's cell than a personal sanctuary. The plus point was the long window, but that was ignored and framed by some very tired curtains. The owner tried to excuse the state of it by claiming it was a blank canvas. Well, if you must leave your buyer a blank canvas, at least make it a clean one. The walls were improved by being painted a soft peach. Then I moved the bed to make better use of the space and made a simple headboard. Textured wallpaper, Lincrusta, was applied to a piece of MDF and then painted silver, a strong contemporary colour. It was repeated in the new bedlinen, contemporary chair and curtains. I chose a pleated blind for the window that pulled upwards to ensure privacy yet allowed in as much light as required. Storage was essential so we made a simple canvas wardrobe to give the idea there was room for something more permanent. As for the poor old plant in the bedroom, I neatly trimmed the partially dead leaves so it didn't look as if it had been hacked to death. With a new lampshade, some cushions for contrast and three small pictures above the bed, it was hard to believe it was the same room.

BEFORE

AFTER

PICTURE CREDITS

Photographs courtesy of TalkBack/Channel 5 except the following:

Amtico: 90, 91

Bill Stephenson: 27

Bisque: 76

Brume: 57

Chris Ridley: 27, 73, 79, 85. 98-99, 103, 108, 112–113, 114, 131, 139, 140–141, 145, 149, 153, 158–159

Christopher Wray Lighting: 96, 97

Clyde Combustions Ltd: 77

Crown Decorative Products ltd: 26, 27, 42, 43, 51, 60, 61, 73, 77, 84, 101, 137

Danico: 97

Dave Young: 87, 112, 118, 130, 144, 148

Hilarys: 70

Ikea: 22, 23

Lee Hind/Living ETC/IPC Syndication: 47, 55

Marshall Tufflex Window Systems: 33, 34, 35

Michelle Jones: 43

Natural Flooring Company: 90, 91

Robert Harding: 38, 39, 52, 53, 82–83, 110–111, 116-117, 122–123, 150-151, 154–157

Stuart Chorley: 129

T. Young/Living ETC/IPC Syndication: 46

Scott del Amo/Cobra ltd: 100, 133, 136